Night Café:

The Amorous Notes of a Barista

Other books from EyeCorner Press
http://eyecornerpress.com/

COARCTATE: ANTIGONE'S RETURN AND SELECTED POEMS
by MARK DANIEL COHEN
(drama, poetry, criticism, August 2010)

PULVERIZING PORTRAITS
by CAMELIA ELIAS
(poetry criticism, January 2010)

JAGGED TIMELINE
by ROBERT GIBBONS
(poetry, bilingual ed. with an intro by B. Sørensen, December 2009)

BETWEEN GAZES: FEMINIST, QUEER, AND 'OTHER' FILMS
by CAMELIA ELIAS
(criticism, March 2009)

PASSION SPENT: LOVE, IDENTITY, AND REASON IN E.A. POE
by BENT SØRENSEN
(criticism, July 2008)

FEDERMAN FRENZY
by CAMELIA ELIAS, ed.
(criticism, October 2008)

FIVE FACES OF DERRIDA
by BENT SØRENSEN, ed.
(criticism, July 2008)

ÅRSTIDER I SKEPTIKERENS HIMMEL
by VALERIU BUTULESCU
(aforismer; udvalgt og oversat af C.Elias & B. Sørensen, July 2008)

EIGHT SENSES PLUS TWO
by CAMELIA ELIAS
(poetry, July 2008)

UNTITLED
by CAMELIA ELIAS, ed.
(criticism, July 2008)

NIGHT CAFÉ:

THE AMOROUS NOTES OF A BARISTA

GRAY KOCHHAR-LINDGREN

INTRODUCTION BY
BENT SØRENSEN

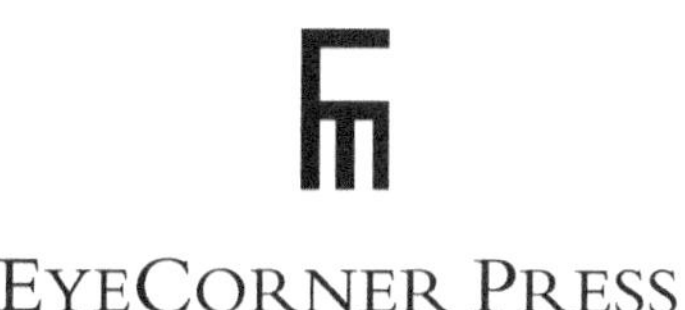

EyeCorner Press

Night Café: The Amorous Notes of a Barista

Published by EYECORNER PRESS, September 2010

ISBN: 978-87-92633-01-9

Cover design and layout: Camelia Elias

The text has been typeset in Bembo

Printed in the US and UK

MENU

Acknowledgements

The Café Orphée, with its elegant hotel, is a very real and quite enticing place in Regensburg (http://www.hotel-orphee.de/). Earlier versions of the material on Vincent Van Gogh and Walter Benjamin have been published in *Respiro* (www.respiro.com) and the *Café Irreal* (http://cafeirreal.alice-whittenburg.com/). Also, and as always, enduring thanks to Duncan and Kanta, who know both the face of the mountains and the darkness of the subterranean caves.

For Robert and Sylvia Hrdina

One More Cup of Coffee

---

for the Road

by Bent Sørensen

Introduction

As one prepares to depart for somewhere, anywhere, elsewhere—for instance Turin, where Nietzsche went mad and embraced horses (having abstained from coffee for years); or London, the mother lode of coffeehouse culture, where the distinction between public and private was first seeded (and where simultaneously, as witnessed by Pepys, its ultimate breech formed at its very inception); or Seattle, the epicenter of the latest flavor of American imperialism (latte, mocha or frappaccino?)—one could do worse than picking up a small volume of essays limning the inescapable condition of every departure merely being a preparation for the ultimate departure and return. Exactly such a volume is Gray Kochhar-Lindgren's coffee-occasioned musings on art, literature and philosophy, *Night Café,* which you now hold in your hands.

I recommend approaching the volume armed with a mug of Café Noir made on a Danish state-of-the-art French press by Bodum, while listening to the languid female voices on Vancouver-based label Nettwerk's luxurious double CD-set, one volume entitled *Slowbrew*, the other *Percolator*—or, for the later chapters, Maxim Vengerov's selections from the virtuoso salon music of Vienna, performed on his 1727 Stradivarius, The Ex-Kreutzer – an instrument once owned and played by Rodolphe Kreutzer, French virtuoso of the late 18th C., who came to Vienna both to sample the coffee drinks (tantalizingly listed in their multifarious glory and variety by Gray within) and play at Court, and there incidentally met Beethoven who dedicated a violin sonata to him (Kreutzer, however, detested the work and found it unplayable…)

Filled to the brim with poetry and music, Gray's volume reminds us of how thinking and creativity often requires a stimulus from the outside to flow freely. Hemingway, Rilke and Schnitzler are but a few of the authors we encounter in these essays where the voices of their texts intermingle with the sound of Orpheus's lyre in the din of the round-tabled 'penny university' of Gray's making. The reader is free to add other remembered voices to the choir, as she follows the meandering paths of thinking and sensing carved out by the little book. For me, perhaps unavoidably, the poets preoccupied with rituals of departure speak the loudest—Leonard Cohen, as the Wandering Jew seeking final repose, from *The Book of Longing,* now re-christened *The Book of Blue Coffee:*

better than coffee
is blue coffee
which you drink
in your last bath
or sometimes waiting
for your shoes
to be dismantled

Or, Bob Dylan, a no-less-Wandering Man preoccupied with the eternal feminine, stalling his farewell with "one more cup of coffee, 'fore I go to the valley below." There is eternal return awaiting these fine gentlemen, as indeed Orpheus found out and Nietzsche reiterated.

Setting is all-important, as Gray reminds us from the onset, enumerating the places his narrative persona, the nomadic barista of the volume's subtitle, has been to already, currently lounges in, or plans to visit in future. The list of sites, not coincidentally, shares many elements of Gray's own personal geographies, both those of location and of the imagination: Whidbey Island, Seattle, London, Paris, Vienna and Regensburg, nose pointing finally toward Hong Kong.

In his landmark volume of essays, the master of Greek lore and poetry Guy Davenport reminds us that "The imagination has a history, as yet unwritten, and it has a geography, as yet only dimly seen. History and geography are inextricable disciplines. They have different shelves in the library, and different offices at the university, but they cannot get along for a minute without consulting the other. Geography is the wife of history, as space is the wife of time" (*The Geography of the Imagination,* p. 4). In the *Night Café* essays Gray quietly illustrates the truth of Guy's claims, taking us on a sweeping, historically informed journey through the loci where coffee visually, legibly and audibly intersected with human development (for instance, playfully suggesting that the common geographical origin of the sacred bean and the upright, tool-wielding homo is not mere coincidence). Focal characters often step into the center of Gray's short meditations to consult with us on the consequences of the Nietzschean will-to-power, which Gray playfully pursues as it permutates from will-to-espresso to will-to-death. These characters are more often than not the tragic ones: Benjamin, whose suicide in Port-Bou may well have been premature; Ernest Hemingway, whose final blast in Ketchum, Idaho may well have been pathetically overdue; Vincent the Starry-Eyed, whose madness may have been purified by too much rationality in the face of decay and dark night of the human soul; Rilke, the Romantic-in spite-of himself, who could not take a lesson from Lou Salomé (nor, by the way, would Nietzsche who considered her his pupil...); and not least the God of Song, Orpheus, who could not leave well enough alone, but looked behind and learned that ultimately the song sings the singer...

A key theme in Gray's book is conflict, arbitration and the potential for solution (via coffee and reason) of the many conflicts—imagined and real—that run through human history. The players in the drama of history are often divided by their relationship with the bean, he claims—neatly placing the power-mad, control-hungry dictators and all those who think that prohibition of the brown liquid is possible and desirable on the side of the schmucks and losers deservedly left on the trash heap of history (in one particularly pleasing instance "Sliced in two at the waist. Chop, chop") among the used-up grounds...

Gray has faith in the power of the spoken word, of reason and argument, the Hegelian dialectics—and, on occasion, technological reason, when put to noble pursuits such as the perfect espresso engine. Yet, a wide streak of hauntology runs through his writing (and even the good Hegel cannot appear without being accompanied by the black Dog of Night) and he cannot escape his fascination with particularly significant loci, such as Chernobyl's abandoned coffee-house where "the ghosts come only to meet other ghosts." Gray joins the list of those who remain to bear witness of the past and its glories, blind alleys, mistakes, and crimes—a function artists and philosophers alike must fulfill for the benefit of future generations, if indeed such are to exist.

The chief lament of these essays concerns the demise of the university as a site of negotiation of sense and opinion. The coffee shop as the open and free 'penny university' where all are welcome and respected for their input and willingness to participate (rather than their ability to pay and their eagerness to conform) is offered up as a way forward, and who can fail to be seduced by the utopian principle of hope Gray's barista—tongue only halfway in cheek—espouses: "If only universities had remained available for the clink of a few coins and housed in cafés around the world!" We would have had "a community of steamed epistemo-lovers, a poetics of the café that married the most rigorous mathematics to the most voluptuous architectures of taste." The world would certainly have been a better place!

Gray's sense of whimsy and his contagious enthusiasm for the oblique approach in the search of knowledge and insight are traits that suffuse his writing as well as his teaching. I have had the privilege of witnessing him teach cultural studies 'live', seeing him empty his pockets—laying it all on the table, literally as well as figuratively speaking—inviting eager students to read the latest additions to his collection of hotel key cards, seeking the glitch in any technology or machinery ('cause growth occurs in the cracks). Similarly, in these essays, Gray asks us implicitly to pick our favorite sentences (as he does in class—this being the students' chief home-work) and explain to him just why we like them.

I, for one, appreciated learning about the weirdness of Sartre's penchant for balloons, and I agree with Gray that generally speaking far too little work has been done on the interrelation between philosophy and meteorology—just as I agree with Derrida that we need to know much more about the sex lives of the philosophers—with the possible exception of Sartre's... I also very much enjoyed the flight of fancy involved in what I can only refer to as Gray doing an Italian job on Hemingway, imaginatively inserting him in the canon of Italian poets; wandering with Gray and Benjamin through the urban labyrinths of *The Arcades Project;* savoring the Danish connection in Schnitzler's *Dream Narrative* (knowing already about his involvement in the nascent Danish film industry and his love of the Danish beaches and Victorian beach hotels north of Copenhagen—but that is a story I want to share with Gray when next we meet, just as we'll have a nice etymological discussion of the third, metaphorical meaning of *Einspänner* (lone wolf!) —which lends yet another dollop of goodness to the tension between the two meanings Gray mentions ("one-horse carriage" and "black coffee in a glass with a freshly whipped cream").

But now I invite you along on the journey to, through and beyond the *Night Café* of Gray's imagination. These amorous notes show a deep, dark passion for philosophy (which would then be philo-philosophy, I suppose), literature and art—as well as an ardent love of the dispeller of all worries, the drink whose ingestion—and the ensuing thoughts—Gray convinces us amounts to a Hell of a lot more than a mere hill of beans.

⋆ ⋆ ⋆

Oh Coffee, you dispel the worries of the great, you point the way to those who have wandered from the path of knowledge… Take time in your preparations for coffee and God will be with you and bless you and your table.

Sheik Ansari Djerzeri Hanball Abd-al-Kadir

Welcome to the Café Orphée

I am a nomadic barista. Beginning my career at the Useless Bay Coffee House on Whidbey Island, I graduated to the Vivace in Capitol Hill, a neighborhood of bricklayers, entrepreneurs, bums, librarians, and artists just up the hill from Seattle's famous Pike Place Market. There I apprenticed myself to masters and began to learn the delicate strength of the foam-art of cappuccino, how to make the shape of a heart, a spade, an arabesque that could never be duplicated and vanished at the first touch of a tongue. The years and the lattes flew by and I have now come of age as a barista, a businessman, and as an amateur historian of the Divine Bean. I have taken a six month sabbatical to wander, sipping and writing, through London, Paris, Vienna, and, now find myself here at the Café Orphée in Regensburg, where, each night I'm settling in by the window for a stint of reflection before I hit the road once again. I have a week and then I'll fly from Munich to Hong Kong, where I have been invited to set up The Coffee Emporium on Hau Wo Street in Kennedy Town.

The Orphée is a classic café accompanied by an exquisite hotel. (I am, however, staying with old friends in their flat on Alte

Nürnberger Strasse.) It has, in fact, become quite famous in its own small way since Regensburg was declared a UNESCO World Heritage Site and Wim Wenders, who directed my favorite film, sang its praises on the Orphée website (http://www.hotel-orphee.de/index.htm). As he says:

> Nowhere else is it more pleasurable to pause for a bit and sweetly do nothing. A certain attitude to life is inextricably linked to these places: A Lightness of Being, yet one containing a certain measure of reflection and contemplation; right in the midst of the world and yet far from it.

There's more, but I'll leave that for you to explore. Outside the café, fitted to the stone wall, is a small incised metal plaque.

> Ancient brewery grounds with brewing room, storage cellars and lounge (1896) of the Fürstliche Brauerei Thurn und Taxis. In the second half of the 20th century the gypsy king Aloys Finkelstein-Korntheur—who had fled from Hungary—opened a cafe-brasserie with accommodation and a serving of meals in the French tradition.

There is a history here—and much has been written about the Thurn und Taxis family of Holy Roman Empire postal service fame—and there is an ambience of contemplation and the quietly erotic.

I have a week. I have my notes. I'll sit by the window and do what I can before heading to the Hong Kong. There is, of course, no such thing as the café without coffee or of coffee without the café. They form a constellation. You will recall Talleyrand's memorable verse. Coffee, he said, is:

Noir comme le diable,
Chaud comme l'enfer,
Pur comme un ange,
Doux comme l'amour.

The café, and the hot coffee served in so many ways, is poetry, history, and politics. It is black as the devil and as hot as hell; pure as an angel and as sweet as love. It is all of these things. I'll start, tonight, with a simple *café au lait* and work my way around to more baroque offerings as the week passes. The winter is hard upon us and the Danube is frozen solid along the edges. I am glad I am inside, looking out the window onto Untere Bachgasse, my own reflection and that of the other patrons are as visible in the glass as the passerbys outside, bundled against the cold. I am glad I have my old journal and a new pen, a hot cup of coffee steaming by my side.

1

Café

The history of the café, that most noble of institutions, is a well-known fable that begins at the Kiva Han in Constantinople in 1453. Those crafty old Venetians brought the elixir from there into the west, where it underwent trial by fire in the Secret Chamber of Cardinals and was then baptized as a good Christian drink by Clement VIII, although the sources differ as to which Pope it was who actually took a hankering to the dark brown beauty of the secret drink of the infidels. By 1652, the coffeehouse had passed into merry olde England and was baptized with the name of the "penny university," as that's what a cuppa cost, and it always initiates passionate, if not always erudite, debate back and forth across the table.

And, just as with the foolish shortsightedness of Pope Clement VIII's advisors, Charles II in England, and Frederick of Prussia, the governor of Mecca tried to ban the substance for fear it would undermine his rule. The Sultan, being far wiser than the governor concerning the power of coffee, had the impudent man executed, probably sliced in two at the waist. Chop, chop. Coffee haters have always abounded, for there is always fear of freedom and fear of a convivial gathering, but they have always, everywhere, lost their ground. Given the ineluctable movement of the freedom to enjoy one's cup in one's own time, one's own place, and with companions of one's own choosing, it is a shame that such violent disputes still occur. When will we learn?

If only universities had remained available for the clink of a few coins and housed in cafés around the world! Our scholars could hold forth with equal authority on a dusty roadside under a tin roof or in the most chi-chi TopSpot in Berlin. There would be a constant exchange of knowledge hungry students between east and west, north and south, between the lands where frappaccino rules and those where Nescafé, brewed in an instant, sets the standards. The smooth pleasures of the bean would replace the jagged edges of ideology and the great arguments of the age would concern the grounds for the essential virtues of the various drying processes and whether the Yemeni or Colombian bean has precedence in the new networks of taste.

Instead of suffering in its current pitiful, desiccated condition—dominated as it is by abstraction, profit, and so-called utility—the knowledge generated in the university would be something voluptuously aromatic, a perfume that awakens the longing of the soul. Philosophy would be as delicious as a warm *pain au chocolat* just out of the oven, physics an investigation of the equations of the cool cream as it swirls elegantly, like a newly forming galaxy, into the hotter coffee. We would do longitudinal studies of the sociology of round or rectangular tables. There would be a great clamor for seminars on the aesthetics of café chairs and the economics of chocolate shavings, the spirituality of cappuccino—named, of course, after the robes of the Capuchins—and the psychology of the choice between cloth or paper napkins.

The barista would need an advanced degree and all the visual artists would have to pass an exam by painting a work lit only by candlelight shimmering in the coffeehouse mirrors. Rembrandt and Manet would be proud of their ability to handle reflected light. And what is true illumination but light reflected and refracted, the lights of a café late at night reflected in the mirrors, in the windows, off the lacquer glaze of the tables, and in the eyes of all the lovers with their fingers resting lightly on their coffee cups?

Everything would be sensual and shared as we developed, as a community of steamed epistemo-lovers, a poetics of the café that married the most rigorous mathematics to the most voluptuous architectures of taste. Professorships would be granted only to those masters of the imagination who demonstrated the greatest flair in frothing or in designing the next-generation coffee-maker. All students would get free tuition, a bed in a dry room, a set of oil paints, biscotti, and ten cups a day. All concrete and brick buildings would be torn down and replaced by Bauhaus or art-deco, postmodern *ne plus ultra,* or tropical bungalows.

All the university cafés would be open to the weather when the weather is fine and snug and warm when the weather turns sour. White clouds in a high blue sky, with the breeze coming in from the sea, from over the mountains to the east. Even a light rain and the occasional snow flurry. We'd all become peripatetics, strolling between different seminar tables in the House of Language and between cities as we absorbed the different styles of learning at the renowned Café Uni.

But one of those penny universities, alas, was Edward Lloyd's and you know the fate of that surname in London business circles. Protecting ships and the knees of athletes. Green baize tables all in a row. As the 17th century headed toward its close, already the modern university was taking a dim, but visible shape. You know the rest, once the University of Berlin decides its destiny in 1810 after the tragically missed opportunity at Jena. Long before that tragedy occurred, however, the coffeehouse had crossed the channel to what would become arguably the Café Capital—though the Viennese also have a strong argument for that honor—until recently, when, perhaps, the final decline has begun. In Paris, the franchised chains are encroaching everywhere and nothing, nothing at all, is safe from the economies of scale.

But the City of Light will not give up without a fight—I pray for victory—and it still has its private pleasures: Hediard's, for example, in its singular location on the Place de la Madeleine since 1854. It's a lovely shop full of the aroma of mixed spices, the walls lined with wine bottles and jars of jams and mustards. The floors are always well-polished and the clerks immaculately dressed. I find it comforting to step into this quiet oasis from the noisy bustle of the streets that are teeming with rabid shoppers headed like greyhounds out of the box toward Printemps and the Galeries Lafayette. That, after all, is why the good M. Haussmann razed and rebuilt the city along those wide boulevards. Shop until you drop was his slogan, since the ruling elites, like other elites in other countries, understood shopping to be essential to national stability.

I pass by all the other temptations that beckon to the senses at Hediard's—and there are many—and head straight for the coffee. The store boasts varieties of beans from all over the world, stored in burlap-lined barrels, just waiting for a hand to come and caress the rounded bean, let the coffee run through the slightly spread fingers like an ancient *vita aurum,* those mythical waters of golden richness. I buy a few pounds of Blue Mountain—to be reserved for consumption only among friends—pick up the certificate of origin, and then step back outside into the noisy maelstrom of money-lust. Coffee is a doorway into another space, a place of sensual abundance and intellectual lucidity. It is a threshold, which is why Orpheus is our patron and Hediard's is one of his many temples. A gust; an aroma: the god.

The story of coffee intoxicates me, makes my head spin. I have to hold on to the edges of the table to keep from fainting. But you know what that is like, to be swept up into ecstasy. Once again, as with the Pope's first sip and ensuing decree, it was over coffee that the so-called east came into contact with the so-called west. This thread of gold and blood runs through the whole history of coffee, the true universal of post-Kaldic modernity, but which has yet to be recognized as such. When it is, when it finally comes into its rightful place, then and not until then will there be genuine and lasting peace in the world.

Conflict will naturally remain—that, emerging from our simian past, is human nature—but the disputes will be between those who favor the French press and the *aficionados* of the drip brew, between the Espresso Masters Guild and the Secret Society of Mocha Latte Lovers. They will declare war with a sneer across a table and a napkin violently thrown down in challenge, and all such wars will be settled by a publicly judged taste test. All victories and all defeats will be celebrated with a rambunctious Feast of Pastries until all fall into unconsciousness from the sheer exhaustion of eating Napoleons and petit fours.

But that is a history yet to come. In the history that we know to date—that holds us fast and forces us to make up new tales—it was the Dutch, that tiny but indomitable nation of merchants, that provided the hinge between both east and west, as well as north and south. The first part of the tale, as delightful as *The Arabian Nights,* begins in Mocha, a Yemeni port that sits at the mouth of the Red Sea and the Gulf of Aden, just to the south of Saudi Arabia. Suicide attacks on the U.S. Fleet and high mountain villages full of radical tribalists get most of the press today, but in the long arc of history coffee will be victorious over the petty politics of this or that Empire, all of which come, take themselves far too seriously, and then go.

The port from which we get the beatific "mocha" is also known variously as Al-Mokha, Al-Makha, Al-Mukha, and Al-Mukh (and undoubtedly other names as well, as every city has many more names than it requires). Coffee, sweet from the mountains, had been drunk for centuries in that part of the world, until, in 1690, a coffee plant was smuggled from Mocha by the cunning Dutch, who then—in the finest colonial fashion of the times—began the first large-scale commercialization of the wondrous bean in Ceylon and Java. The bean, a simple form of the desire for company and the pleasure of a slight buzz, became a booming business.

Cup of Java? That comes from those coffee plantations administered, often quite brutally, by the Dutch in the East Indies, and forged into a phrase first brought to the US during the California Gold Rush because "Java" was stamped on the burlap bags. Coffee, tea, cotton, opium, sneakers, cheap electronics, pants and shirts, car parts. Goods moving around the world from the poor to the rich. It's been that way for a very long time.

In 1602, the Dutch had chartered the *Verenigde Oostindische Compagnie,* the Dutch East Indies Company, a conglomerate with branches based in Amsterdam, Delft, Rotterdam, Enkhuizen, Hoorn, and Middelburg, a huge and thriving company that kept booming along until 1799. The world's first multinational, the VOC had a run of two centuries, a long time in which to perfect the arts of commerce, the forced labor of slavery, and war. Plantations and death, all for the little bean that would enrich the shareholders in Holland.

There's now a VOC Café at Prins Hendrikkade 94, in Amsterdam, and another branch of this multifoliate history runs through a certain Eugene Dubois, a Dutchman who traveled in 1887 to East Java to dig around for human fossil remains at Trinil, on the mouth of the Solo River. He found a skull cap, upper jaw molar, and a femur, naming his find *Pithecanthropus Erectus,* "upright walking ape-man." In Germany, just another little delicious tidbit, the main Java Site is called *Kaffee und Kuchen.* That's for computer programming, mind you, so "Java" has migrated from place, to a drink, to a complex software program. Perhaps there is a secret hidden away here, something about the way things, or at least their meanings, change?

But I am digressing. Sometimes I think that all we ever do is digress, until that moment when we breathe our last and no longer—at least one might presume—have the taste for either *robustica* or *arabica.* On the other hand, perhaps heaven itself is a small café tucked away on a street much like the Untere Bachgasse, the Boul Mich, Wellington Street in Hong Kong, Taksim Square in Istanbul, and the other altars around the world dedicated to the service of the life of the bean.

But back to those ambitious Dutch, for pride always precedes the fall. In 1713, they made the grave mistake of giving Louis XIV a coffee bush as a gift, a small and seemingly innocent present that, just as the theft of mocha from Al-Mukha, changed the course of history. In 1723, Gabriel Mathieu do Clieu—some say a naval officer and some an infantry commander—stealthily invaded the *Jardin des Plantes,* stole a coffee plant, and then transported it across the stormy Atlantic to Martinique, where it was planted, did rather well for itself, and within 50 years provided more than 90% of the coffee in the world. There is also the little deception involved in the way the magical plant makes its way into Brazil, but I won't go into that. Think about it. By the end of the 18th century, coffee had made its way into Africa, the Middle East, Europe, the Caribbean, and then to Central and South America. And all because of a stolen kiss, a little theft here and a little chicanery there, and a great deal of power politics everywhere.

2

Evolution

The global bean, roasted and triumphant. The bean, rampant on a field of scarlet and gold. Heraldic, flaming. The bean, almost as small as the mustard seed. I have been spouting the origins of the tale of the magic of coffee, which are in fact shrouded in impenetrable obscurity, wrapped in layer upon layer of legend. Who knows where it will end, if it will end? All we can do is pass the legend from hand to hand, mouth to mouth, ear to ear. We are all places of passage, all mutations of the evolutionary force that drives the world as a will to the perfect espresso, the frothy cappuccino.

Although the highly praised and highly intoxicated Kaldi, that famous goat-herder, or the nomadic Gallas are usually given the honor of the first divine sip (or chew) of coffee, I am convinced that the brown brew made its appearance much, much earlier in human history. After all, in order to come down from the trees or out from their leafy jungle nests, our early kin had to start growing a larger brain and reorient to bipedalism. Something, a chemical miracle as it were, had to trigger this transformation and that, obviously, was coffee. Not a mocha latte with legs, but just one berry after the next ground up between those powerful jaws, triggering the long slow enlargement of the frontal cortex that would lead, eventually, to the Kiva Han, the Procope, Edward Lloyd's, Il Maestro Gaggi, and that little shop on Pike Place Market in Seattle that has now spread around the world. It is not, let me say immediately, that we are the pinnacle of evolutionary history, for such history has no pinnacle. It's just that we are a very dense, very intense part of the network of miracle that is history.

Philosophers like to talk about the self-dividing Idea that begins the serpentine march of history. Total rubbish. It's the bean, that hard little nugget of material magic, that gets the show on the road. I call it the Coffee Evolutionary Hypothesis (CEH). The bean after all, like the earliest hominids, comes from those same African gorges and highlands that brought all of us to this state called modernity. This is the Argument of Propinquity. Lucy herself enjoyed her short happy life around 3,000,000 years ago in Hadar, on the river just north of Addis Ababa. The diggers haven't yet found firm evidence of coffee that far back, but my money is that one of those intrepid, patient excavators will one of these days hit pay dirt in Hadar, Laetoli, or Olduvai. With the advance of DNA analyses and the newest dating methods, as well as a new crop of enthusiastic paleoarcheologists, the odds are rising.

Time unscrolled itself ever so slowly, meandering this way and that like a sluggish brown river. Not much happened in those eons upon eons of days and nights in terms of events that one could separate out as event. The sun rose and set; the moon rose and set; the stars rose and set. Clouds gathered and dispersed over the millions of years. Seas formed and dried into fossil-strewn mountains. Hominids, with an expanding range of hoots and chitters, with hand gestures both small and large, wandered across the savannas and deserts searching for food and water, forming small bands, and producing little hominids that, ever so slowly, were changing their faces and the face of the earth. Hominids died, their flesh becoming carrion food and dust, while their bones settled into a long wait for the arrival of the fossil-hunters.

But things were beginning to occur that punctuated the seamlessness of that strange animal becoming human. Stone-flake tools were made about 2.5 million years ago and fire, one of the greatest mysteries, was domesticated some half a million years ago. And then, miraculously, we enter into that period called the Upper Paleolithic—let's say about 40,000-15,000 years ago—when Sapiens and Neandertals, the remains of which were first discovered in Germany at the Feldhofer Cave, were battling for the grand prize of survival. We won that battle, but only so far. The game's not over, not by a long shot, and we may join our heavy-browed kinfolk yet, perhaps in the disturbingly near future.

There is, everyone agrees, an almost inexplicable burst of creativity when complexity explodes on all fronts during the Upper Paleolithic. Fishhooks, needles, harpoons, snowshoes, bows and arrows. People—what else can we call them?—burying their dead with grave goods. There must have been some sort of ritual attached. That extraordinary flowering of art at Lascaux, Altamira, Chauvet. Those red handprints deep in the darkness of the earth. And, who knows how, the emergence of language. Speaking, mourning, planning, hoping, joking, imagining.

Now, at last, time could occur in its fullness for these odd creatures. Of course, as with Herr Kolschitzky and his Camel Bags of Turkish Coffee—who is said to have first brought the bean to the west after the defeat of the Ottoman at Vienna—there is great debate about all of these issues. But no one doubts that a surge of creativity occurred in the Upper Paleolithic, as it had earlier when the chimp-sized brain of australopithecines almost doubled a couple of million years ago and then, around half a million, jumped again.

What caused these leaps of the human imagination? We have already established the Argument from Propinquity, pointing out that Lucy and the coffee plant are both from what we now call Ethiopia. Second, as we all know, caffeine is a stimulant, so the Argument from Stimulation simply states that since there have been leaps in our brainpower, there must be a cause for those leaps. QED: coffee is the primordial catalyst. Third, many species did not make it through the flaming hoops of survival. The Neandertals, our close cousins, as developed and as long-lived as they were, nonetheless couldn't make it out of their European caves. They just couldn't adjust to modern life. Since we survived, and we have coffee, and they didn't survive, they must not have developed the habit of a morning brew. This, we might say, is the Argument from Evolutionary Failure. And, finally, with the majestic leap ahead of the Upper Paleolithic, which leads more or less directly to Starbucks, we have established the Argument from Complexity, which is closely related to Propinquity, Stimulation, and Evolutionary Failure.

Four Impeccable Arguments that prove, beyond a shadow of a doubt, that human evolution would not have occurred, or would certainly not have occurred as it has, without the divine bean. Pure spirit manifested as pure materiality. B u t while the characteristics of coffee culture are identical to those needed to survive and make an evolutionary leap—stimulus, adaptability, sociability, intelligence, innovation, and habit—there is one important difference. Our distant relatives had to learn, over millions of years, to stand up on their own two feet and take to the road. And, while this is still seen in some Italian espresso bars and American fastfood joints, the true habitués of the café have had to learn, once again, to slow down and sit. They have had to learn, rather arduously at times, the art of patience, a willingness to wait. But as we leave prehistory behind, with its rotund Venus figures who must have loved their pastries morning, noon, and night, and move back into our own world, let us make a nod of gratitude in their direction. For their courage and perseverance, their indomitable spirits, their love of primitive coffee has put us on our way, given us the chance, for a wisp of a moment, to be.

The more we know about something, and the more that we love it, then the more we want to talk about it. The more we want to talk about it, the greater the sophistication required by the innovations of our language. We make our world through enlarging the range of our chitchat, thus proving another reason why the café is indispensable to the expansion of world civilization. The coffee klatch, which so often becomes a kvetch, is the primary example of the workings of metaphysics, which is why all those eggheads in the Vienna Circle were such knuckleheads. They had forgotten that metaphysics leads not to empty and meaningless statements, to pure nonsense, but directly to the café.

The *Tractatus* should have been listened to as a symphony, not as a dull and numbered list, and about that which we cannot speak we should certainly not keep silent. These men spent far too much time in musty old libraries and laboratories, and not nearly enough time with women in cafés. Truth, logic, positivism? That would get them nowhere in the flirtatious play of wit constantly at work in the whole of Vienna. Freud, of course, did not forget wit and his famous couch is but an alternative form of the café for women of a certain class. We must, after all, be able to talk about sex with someone. Why not a stranger with a beard, nodding off to dreamland while pretending to take notes on our all-so-important family history. But, thankfully, the logical positivists one and all are fading into the past of the greatest error, while the *Einspänner* continues to make its robust rounds.

Regardless of the exact facts of the Kolschitzky Affair—although Teply's evidence seems to me incontrovertible—coffee is positioned as the pivot of World History, the bean that marks the leap ahead in human evolution, the presumed salvation of the West from the evil incursions of the barbarian East. Christendom is preserved on the field of battle at the same time that the elixir of coffee first drips onto the insatiable palate of the West. This, obviously, is the dull tale told only from the side of the Europeans, since the Ottoman Empire had long been enjoying the pleasures of coffee as a stimulant to conversation, a love-potion to increase the pleasures of the bed, a medicinal brew that could cure all ills, and even, for the Sufis, as a catalyst to a mystical union with the divine. As Sheik Ansari Djerzeri Hanball Abd-al-Kadir intoned all the way back in 1587:

> Oh Coffee, you dispel the worries of the Great, you point the way to those who have wandered from the path of knowledge. Coffee is the drink of the friends of God, and of His servants who seek wisdom...No one can understand the truth until he drinks of its frothy goodness. Those who condemn coffee as causing man harm are fools in the eyes of God. Coffee is the common man's gold, and like gold it brings to every man the feeling of luxury and nobility...Take time in your preparations for coffee and God will be with you and bless you and your table. Where coffee is served there is grace and splendor and friendship and happiness. All cares vanish as the coffee cup is raised to the lips. Coffee flows through your body as freely as your life's blood, refreshing all that it touches: look you at the youth and vigor of those who drink it. Whoever tastes coffee will forever forswear the liquor of the grape. Oh drink of God's

> glory, your purity brings to men and women only well-being and nobility.

What else can be said? Drink and be blessed. Splendor, friendship, happiness. The frothy goodness of coffee gives us truth and grace, the very glory of God.

The bean is also the highway and crossroads of the globe, for it is the great equalizer. Around the globe it has traveled and continues to travel, bringing with it the ancient spices of the café conversations of the great cultures. The early *homo caffeinnius* in the shade of the baobab tree; the Yemenis setting sail from Al-Mukha; the Turks in Vienna; the Dutch in Java; the French and Portuguese in Brazil; the Americans all over the place in more recent, but also passing, history. North to south and east to west, coffee wends its way, often backed by the force of arms, but, always following the path of desire. Money, sex, and coffee: the great triumvirate.

In hindsight and with foresight, I would rather be governed by the Imperial Coffee Proconsul that by any other form of the long arm of capitalism. I would also recommend that all those now fighting each other be required by officials dressed regally in forest-green uniforms with gold braid on the shoulders to meet at the coffee shop at the Sacher for as long as it took to come to a mutual resolution. There, they would gather daily in the great rose-windowed Hall of Disputation and argue in the most rarefied scientific discourse over the water temperature, the type of grind, the best roasting methods, the agronomy of the bean, the proportions, and their descriptions of the taste of a range of coffees—always the most difficult since this takes us into the realm of aesthetics where *de gustibus est non disputandem*—in order to practice their skills of conflict resolution. The acidity is too imperious. Smooth as caramel. Fruity. Graced with the scent of nuts. Lingers like lime sorbet with a twist of mint on the tongue. No one would be allowed to go home until agreement had been reached and all could shake hands with a renewed respect for the talents and tongues of the other, as well as an acknowledgement of the difficulties that all faced with their surly and ungrateful constituents back home.

There are, as you would guess, as many schools concerning the arts and sciences of coffee as there are sects of religious zealots. As Michael Griffin, who is only one of the thousands of the *philosophes du café* that teem in our midst, has said: "A perfect espresso is more of a concept than an actuality and the beauty is that espresso is volatile and difficult. There are so many factors involved in espresso preparation that only a human mind and a passionate heart can begin to understand and control its complexity." Griffin's comment represents a fine exemplar of the idealist-romantic *Kaffee Schule,* but, on another day he can speak with the best of the technicians about coffee agronomy and the debates over the appropriate pH levels.

Espresso, always mixed in the world of becoming, aspires to the perfection of the ideal concept. It is volatile! Explosive! Everything must go right and anything can go wrong. The beans, the roast, the grind, the tamping, the evils of channeling, the heat of the water or the mechanics of the machine. There can be human or mechanical errors, even the level of humidity in the surrounding air, that must be properly accounted for when the cup is brewed.

The perfect cup, of course, is never achieved and yet that only spurs us to try one more time. It is the limit on the horizon of the world. This is what is taught by all the Romantics and even by Kant himself. (See the section on the Ideals of Reason in *The Critique of Pure Reason,* A805-819.) Perhaps this will be the one? Of course, if that event ever occurred and if a perfect drop of espresso ever touched our arched and expectant tongue, the angels would sing a single note and the world would vanish in an instant. No, there is a limit to the approximation of the infinite, a determination that is the condition of the café experience, one that must occur with the brewing of each demitasse of espresso.

The science of espresso, first manifested in the material world by Maestro Achille Gaggi just after the last of the last Great Wars, has certainly been seeping slowly, drop by drop, into the imagination since the raw beans first kept Kaldi awake with his goats in the Abyssinian highlands. (Perhaps Rimbaud was really dealing in coffee rather than arms? I like to think so.) Volatile, indeed. Like human life itself that mutated from the Olduvai Gorge, the great migratory evolution of coffee begins in Africa and spreads, by fits and starts, throughout the entire world. What saturates our lives, and even the very earth itself, more completely than coffee? We are soaked through with this deep brown, earth-brown, elixir. But it takes a millennium or so until coffee departs from its nomadic ways and enters the café. The brewing of history, after all, is an interminable process of roasting. There is always nature; human need, desire, and inventiveness; and a long, slow burning.

3

Painting

The *Night Café* and the *Café de la Terrasse.* I love all of the Van Goghs as they move from the earth browns of the northern paintings to the explosion of those southern colors about which everyone raves in unison, but the two café paintings are particularly dear to me. I have visited the gallery at Yale, the Metropolitan, the National Gallery in Washington, the glass and steel modernism of the Van Gogh in Amsterdam, and the Kröller-Otterlo in the cool greenness of the park simply to look at his painting on canvas.

September 8, 1888. *The Night Café.* This is the café where, as he said, we could go mad or commit a crime. This is the one so different than the *Café de la Terrasse,* with its charm and serene appeal to the life of the night. This is the other night, the night of night from which no light escapes. Rape, murder, suicide. This is the madness within us all, the hand that keeps a loaded gun under the pillow, and the silent voice that never stops crying.

Not the warmth of the appealing radiance of the *Terrasse,* with the people darkly but richly shadowed, drinking together under the awning so as to be simultaneously outside and inside, to feel the breeze make its way down the street to settle in the cypress branches. Those patrons enjoying themselves under the awning wait with an enthusiastic hope, tinged to be sure with the light resignation of melancholy, but their loss is still yet to come. They still believe in love, seduction, and that most hilarious of all words, happiness.

But in the other café, all is already lost. It always has been. This is the place of absolute despair, where the clock has stopped forever, the hands broken. Time is a whore and this café is a dilapidated absinthe bar where the dead women are exchanged for the hard coldness of coin between one dead man and another. These patrons, too, I also know well. Occasionally, we look at each other in some café or another with a slight nod of recognition.

The ghostly Joseph Ginoux, a fellow proprietor, comes toward me like a ghost, floats behind the slanted pool table. The radiant orbs are like the stars come inside, too large for the room. Used glasses and empty bottles on the tables. Everything pointing to the mysterious illumination of the back room. It is a catastrophe of love. Up for three nights running to paint, Van Gogh panted in the delirium brought about by sleeplessness. "The picture is one of the ugliest I have done," he confessed. No argument there. It is ugliness personified, the absence of any trace of the harmony of beauty. Insomniac: giving up everything to paint, to make sure the fatal vision was transferred to paint. Emerged from paint. The nightmare was indeed painted, but not transferred. No doubt it was an attempt to make an escape, to free the self from itself, from the demons of the self. Munch's scream and the torn viscera of Bacon are both born in Van Gogh's canvas. All of these attempts are of necessity failures. There is no escape, no way out of the claustrophobic infinity of painting.

"I have tried," he said. "I have tried to express the terrible passions of humanity by means of red and green." He succeeded. These are not the passions of desire, the lust for life. These are the colors of death, the reds and greens of despair. "The room is blood red and dark yellow with a green billiard table in the middle; there are four lemon-yellow lamps with a glow of orange and green. Everywhere there is a clash and contrast of the most alien reds and greens, in the figure of little sleeping hooligans, in the empty dreary room, in violet and blue." The room is seasickness. Putrescence.

Alien. That's the exact word. Alien: the disgusting foreignness of reds and greens. How is it possible that those cozy tones of the apples and pears from our backyard gardens become signs of the utterly loathsome? The alien itself: that which cannot be incorporated and therefore keeps Vincent up all night, three days running. He tries to sleep during the day. Night and day contaminate each other. "The blood-red and the yellow-green of the billiard table, for instance, contrast with the soft tender Louis XV green of the counter, on which there is a rose nosegay. The white clothes of the landlord, on vigil in a corner of this furnace, turn lemon-yellow, or pale luminous green." The nosegay tells us about the true stench of the place and of the painting, of all bodies. The ruins of humanity, the moment—

sometimes as long as a lifetime and longer—during which everything is skewed and discolored. Violently bruised.

But in an unexpected and inexplicable way, this wreckage of a bar becomes a seed for the future. Vincent connects the *Night Café* with both *The Potato Eaters*—that early depiction, the colors of dirt, of the poor at their parsimonious table—and with *The Sower,* that very late canvas overflowing with the brightness of the man sowing seed in the golden fields. Or is it this one? I'm not really sure, for Vincent was painting sowers almost constantly, from the beginning to the end. Maybe it's the one in which the golden orbicular sun is rising from the dark head of the sower, the dark tree bent diagonally across the canvas.

In a way, all he ever did was sow painting and paint sowing. Some on rocky ground, some on fertile. He has certainly bloomed, like an almond tree, since his death, but one can look and look and still be blind. The paintings, of course, both do and do not explain themselves. They speak and do not speak, although it is never a speech of explanation, never philosophy or science. Art presents itself, nothing more. But I can speculate; I can make a wager.

Both are, after all, pictures of the earth. Vincent wrote to Theo: "You need a certain dash of inspiration, a ray from on high, things not in ourselves, in order to do beautiful things. When I had done those sunflowers, I looked for the opposite and yet the equivalent, and I said—it is the cypresses." Life is closing down for him, but he connects, without transition, the inspiration from heaven—a dash from somewhere beyond ourselves needed to create beauty—with his effort to take the next step after the sunflowers (which now adorn the offices of dentists, hedge fund managers, and insurance moguls). He moves to the cypress, the wavestruck tree of death, but what's most interesting here is his method: he looks for the opposite yet the equivalent.

This is madness itself. Nothing can be simultaneously both the opposite and the equivalent. One or the other, A or B. But not both. Not at the same time. Consider the implications. They are outrageous. But that's what he said; that's what he was looking for. That's what he painted. Sunflowers are the same as, although simultaneously the opposite of, the cypress. The latter is easy to see: the yellow of ripe life and the mixing of black, blue, and green that is death. But equivalence? How can life equal death and vice versa? How can yellow be black? If there is no distinction, there is no painting. There is no story, no life. Night is not day. Everything depends upon making distinctions and on retaining both the law of identity and the law of non-contradiction.

Perhaps it has something to do not with this incomprehensible methodology—but one which was nonetheless effective—but with an altogether other train of thought, with Vincent's associations about the so-called natural and the so-called artificial world. Yet, "I don't know," he wrote with a certain plaintive tone—not being always a pessimist—"I keep thinking that I have it still in my heart to paint someday a bookshop with its frontage yellow and rose, at evening, and black passers-by—it is such an essentially modern subject. Because it seems, imaginatively speaking, such a wellspring of light—I say, there would be a subject that would go well between an olive grove and a cornfield, the seed time of books and prints. I have a great longing to do it, like a light in the midst of darkness." There is, still, the yellow and the black as the evening falls. There is, again, a series of three that involves a frame and an in-between: olives, bookshop, corn.

Sowing. Seed time.

The books and prints are the seed time, all the letters and images disseminated and ready, after a season of incubation during the dead time of winter, ready to burst forth and give rise to the silver-green olive trees and to corn, to ways in which we cultivate the earth so that it will sustain us. Art is sustenance.

Dark-light-dark: a wellspring.

Seed, springs. Modern subjects. A great longing.

The last summer is drawing near for him.

To make, in the face of absolute darkness, the resonantly glowing life, the work of art that bespeaks the great incessant yearning for something more, for something a little bit more. Potatoes, wheat, the sun. The olives and the corn; the never painted bookshop, the color of rose in the evening light. And then this furnace of the *Night Café* in which all is burning and being smelted down in order to be transfigured. It's all in the intensity of the brushwork.

He wrote to Bernard, his painting-companion and friend, that "my night café is not a brothel: it's a café where the night prowlers cease to be night prowlers, since they pass the whole night hanging limply over the tables without prowling at all. Only by chance a doxy happens to bring her fellow along. But entering one evening, I did catch sight unawares of a little group of a chap and a doxy making up after a tiff. The woman was playing the superbly indifferent, the man was billing and cooing. I set myself to paint it from memory, for you, on a small canvas of 4 or 6."

This small canvas is unknown, lost or destroyed. At least that is what the scholars believe. I believe that someone is, at this very moment, savoring its lines in secret. Gauguin reported that in that beautiful, disastrous autumn of '88, Vincent turned suddenly to a wall, a subject he knew something about, and painted with a scrawl:

Je suis sain d'esprit,

Je suis Saint-Esprit.

I am of sound spirit; I am the Holy Spirit. Opposites. Equivalents. And which sunflower, exactly, is it? The 1887 examples, dead, withered and laid open like a cadaver on the table? Or the more famous ones of 1888?

"I often think that the night is more alive and richly colored," he wrote, "than the day." Yes, yes. He knows the night. He is a man of the night. The night enriches the day, mixes an extravagant palette in preparation for the day, holds the remains of the day in abeyance, in preparation.

4
Waiting

I often think of him traveling by train from one of the great cities of the European disaster to another. Berlin to Paris, back and forth, back and forth. I see him sitting in a chair, half in shadows, in the Bibliothèque Nationale to write notes on thousands of index cards with newspaper clippings and photographs piled randomly around him. He walks in the Mediterranean sun and sits, late in the afternoons, on terraces by the sea. After Capri, he is a changed man, for there he has met Asja Lacis, who cuts a one-way street through his heart. He is tired, he thinks about books, he thinks about taking his own life. He knows that Germany is bearing down on him like a relentless locomotive.

Benjamin knows in his bones about the ways in which the specific texture of places inhabits and governs our imaginations. Marseilles, Paris, Naples, Berlin, Port Bou. All illumination depends on place. As he was waiting for someone—*who* does not matter—at the Café des Deux Magots at St.-Germain-des-Pres, he suddenly sees his life whole, as it were, as a diagram in the shape of a kind of labyrinth. How tempted I am to spend the rest of my time writing about labyrinths and those tables at the Deux Magots. And, less than a stone's throw away, the Café de Flore. What an amorous couple, full of passion for one another but always keeping a decorous distance between themselves even as they flutter the awnings of their eyelids at each other.

Unfortunately—but this is somehow typical of him—several years later he misplaced the sheet of paper on which he had drawn the labyrinth of his life. There it is, for once: our life, whole, but then the evil genie strikes and it is all gone. I like, though, to imagine it will one day turn up—just as a photo of Van Gogh by Victor Morin recently turned up at an antique dealer in Massachusetts—somewhere in somebody's attic, hidden away in a book, almost forgotten by history. Almost, but not quite. All the books we've lost forever. Aristotle's treatise on comedy, the 200,000 in Alexandria. Perhaps Benjamin's translation of Proust's *Sodome et Gomorrhe.* The street fires flickering like a snake's tongue at the books thrown into the squares of Berlin.

We owe Sappho, Virgil, Catullus, St Thomas, and Kafka just to a lucky break or to the refusal of good friends to throw manuscripts into fire. Time, after all, is a blind scullery maid sweeping out the room. She gathers all of the objects of history into a pile of trash and tosses them nonchalantly into the always blazing fire. We have to do what we can to pluck the curled and blackening fragments out of the always growing disintegration.

The labyrinth, Benjamin said, has many entrances leading into the interior through what he calls "primal acquaintances."

Again and again throughout our lives we are guided through passageways to certain types of people until "everything contracts to a figure, a symbol." But the configuration of the labyrinth began long before, in the early days of his young adulthood, when he first becomes an initiate into the life of Orpheus. Wandering into the Viktoria Café and the West End Café he admitted that, at the time, he did not yet "possess the passion for waiting without which one cannot thoroughly appreciate the charm of a café."

Passion, in and of itself, would seem to preclude all conceptions of waiting. Doesn't passion want its object *now*? Isn't that what the urgency of passion suggests? No. Passion may, in fact, extend itself over a lifetime of effort. The passion for art, for building a business, for keeping a café from sinking beneath the waves of fashion, code, or commerce. All of these require patient effort over decades.

One has, naturally, occasionally to wait for service and wait for the slow peregrinations of the waiter, interrupted by conversation with all the patrons old and new, to return to one's table at his own, unhurried pace. Sometimes that takes what feels like days. The paper is read, the silver coffee-pot emptied and all one can do is tap one's fingers slowly, as if reflecting, on the table while staring vacuously into the middle distance. This strategy for attention rarely works, especially in the better establishments that do not require a quick turnover to turn a profit.

It is not, however, merely the service for which one learns the art of waiting. Much more importantly, it is learning to wait with patience for the appearance of love, either as the approach of the person whom one doesn't want to look at but cannot help the slight turn of the eyes, or for the experience of the slight energizing flush—of mind, body, and spirit—that compels the pencil to write in the notebook, on the napkin, on the flap of the matchbook. This is why one arrives at midday or after work, places the coat—usually quite worn—on the rack and then sits at the table with an air of receptive expectation that borders very closely on a kind of madness or of absolute indifference.

Benjamin, too, had to learn the art of this waiting. But, as he went about the city, he was learning a great deal more as well. After the Viktoria and West End, Benjamin and his wandering friends moved on to the Princess Café, where he begins to do a kind of playful social history just as he is also beginning to pursue a certain profession of women. Musing about creating a *Physiology of Coffeehouses,* he begins by dividing them into "professional and recreational establishments," although admitting that, in most cases, the two coincide. As his principal example—and one cannot do sociology without the concept of an empirical example—he chose the Romanische Café, which proudly boasted the legendary Richard, a hunchbacked, disdainful, and therefore much-esteemed, waiter. (This is not the last time that he will mention a hunchback.)

The Romanische becomes the Café Megalomania and as the artists withdrew into the shadows, the bourgeois began to take their place, for "one of the most elementary and indispensable diversions of the citizen of a great metropolis, wedged, day in and day out, in the structure of his office and family amid an infinitely variegated social environment, is to plunge into another world, the more exotic the better. Hence the bars haunted by artists and criminals." This is another division: artists and criminals on one hand, the professional classes on the other.

Just as Freud kept unwittingly returning to the red-light district in—where was it? Rome? Athens?—so, too, Benjamin returns to the Princess, designed by Lucian Bernhard with private boxes whose purposes were quite clear. What have private boxes been used for other than to begin, continue, or finalize, an assignation with a friend or with a stranger? I, myself, am adamantly opposed to private boxes in a café, for a café is open space itself. There is deep solitude and privacy here, no doubt about that, but it is always *in view of others.* I am opposed, here in the café, to walls and secrets of the literal sort, for there is always the open secret to deal with, whether through talk, reading, drink, writing, or silence.

Benjamin even returns, through the detour of surrealism in Paris, to the mysteries of the Princess in Berlin. He ruminates that in Breton's description of the bar on the upper floor of the Théâtre Moderne there is something that "brings back to my memory that most uncomprehended room in the old

Princess Café. It was the back room on the first floor, with couples in the blue light. We called it the 'anatomy school'; it was the last restaurant designed for love." The last? Surely not, although every generation believes itself to be the first and the last. In any case, Benjamin had described this scene in *A Berlin Chronicle* as well. The 'anatomy school' is in the "upper story, hung with violet drapery and illuminated with a violet glow, in which many seats were always empty, while on others couples took up as little space as possible." Blues and violets, the colors of passion and the almost incomprehensible.

It is, in fact, at the Princess Café—although in another epoch of his life—where he eventually comes to write the *Origin of German Tragic Drama*. The Princess, drifting like all things down the entropic funnel, eventually became the Café Stenwyk, until finally it deteriorated into a common beerhouse. There is a scale of value as far as architecture, as well as the social function of interiors, goes. The Princess followed the course of Benjamin's life: downhill, toward ruin. And, yet, there is something that resists this ruin as well. There are remains, traces of charcoal slashed across the torn pages of history.

Reflecting on that which remains, he writes that: "Language shows clearly that memory is not an instrument for exploring the past but its theater. It is the medium of past experience as the ground is the medium in which dead cities lie interred. He who seeks to approach his own buried past must conduct himself like a man digging." Language is to memory as earth is to dead cities. Berlin? Paris? Pompeii? Both memory and these cities are buried in the dirt and in words; they must, then, be excavated and brought to the light of the surface.

A common enough image. That is the theater of memory. We work, then, on the theater of language in order to unearth the past? On behalf of what? Not just to know, although surely there is that as well. No, it's fundamentally for the sake of our own freedom. Something about being buried locks energy into place, freezing us into the ground that is interred language, which means it is already in the form of drama with its acts, scenes, imbroglios, murders, and grand finales. It's as if the past is a constellation of frescoes or relief sculptures like those painted on the Villas of Pompeii or like the friezes of the Parthenon. Writing, then, as a form of both burial and resurrection? But with a fine line of distinction, a seismic shift that makes the earth tremble.

By returning time and again to the same site, by meticulously working our way down through the layers of sediment and brushing off the remains with our dental picks and toothbrushes, we are able to discover the "real treasure hidden within the earth: the images, severed from all earlier associations, that stand—like precious fragments or torsos in a collector's gallery—in the prosaic rooms of our later understanding. And, as important as it is to preserve an 'inventory' of our discoveries—to make a list for our bosses and those who are to come—the essential thing is to know the 'dark joy of the place of the finding itself.'"

Place finds and speaks itself through our labors. The archaeology of memory, whether of what we call individual or what we call collective recollection, is a poetic undertaking that can never give us 'history' or 'autobiography' in the form of what Benjamin calls a "narrative of continuous time." Time, whatever it is, eddies and remains without a final equation. The passion for history that is unearthed for the sake of the future, when both are always on the verge of dissolution. And to accomplish this, both turn toward the space of art.

Benjamin, then, turns from the continuous flow of time that underlies most misconceptions of autobiography toward a space of fragments, the broken torso of Apollo. All of those companions who were closest to him in his Berlin days now "steal along its walls like beggars, appear wraithlike at windows, to vanish again, sniff at thresholds like a genius loci, and even if they fill whole quarters with their names, it is as a dead man's fills his gravestone." And he, in his turn, is a wraith for others, for us, for instance. He arrives from Port Bou as an absence who calls for us. *For*—what does that little word mean? So much hinges upon it. For whom do we appear? For whom do we work, here in the café?

And, in any city like Berlin, Amsterdam, or New York, in every small town and along every solitary desert track that winds its way through the night raging with an infinite spray of stars, there are innumerable names whispering to be heard. How does the name of the dead fill a gravestone? It is incised, cut with violence into an adamantine material that will, nonetheless, vanish over time. In a carved, unmarked stone, a certain mark is cut that particularizes the stone. This, the characters say, is *my* grave. Except, of course, that there is at that time no longer any *my*, so the name that was mine refers to myself as I was at the instant before my death. When, in other words, I was living. The cut skin of the stone is a surface where history, art, and nature all meet and say: he or she *was*. The name itself, carved by an indifferent mason working for a buck, indicates an echoing space of images hollowed out by the unique resonance of an entire life.

Oblivion, after all, is the common lot. Berlin, Benjamin claims, has more than other cities of those "places and moments when it bears witness to the dead, shows itself full of the dead." The caul of death settles everywhere, indiscriminately, but Berlin certainly has its share, not only those who have settled comfortably into the city's Friedhofe—courtyards of contentment—but also those of untold numbers who were annihilated with absolute brutality. By fire raining from the sky, by a train ticket to a camp, by a pistol shot to the head, by the endless miasma of hunger. They are all here, gathered into the terrible company of the dead.

All of the images of Berlin, Benjamin continues, "according to the teachings of Epicurus, constantly detach themselves from things and determine our perception of them." The air is thick with spirits emanating from all things and adhering to our vision even as they reconstitute themselves. Bottle, glass, tablecloth, fork, spoon, vest, door...everything is signed by the ghosts. Berlin, especially for him the Berlin of the late 19th century, returns, remaining true to its nature as a ghost, to the fact that history returns to haunt us. We cannot, it seems, be done with it. The past is not past, for it exerts continuous pressure on the contours of the present, an ancient face emerging from the canvas before our eyes.

It was in the winter months of 1932, with a contract from *Die Literarische Welt* in hand, that Benjamin first began to get together the notes that became *The Berlin Chronicle*. But, as was his wont as a restless man, he left Berlin for the sun of Ibiza—via Hamburg and Barcelona—where he walked across the island with the grandson of Paul Gauguin, read Simenon, and drank coffee while staring out at the azure waters of the Mediterranean. Coffee is not inconsequential for his life, for it was by downing innumerable cups of jet black coffee that, with his hands shaking like a grandfather with Parkinson's, that he escaped conscription into the Prussian army during the Great War, thus missing out on the grand experience of total mobilization. Who knows? Perhaps he would have survived, had another life, never tried to cross the Spanish border. We all wonder that, about ourselves, and none of us ever has the chance to put our curiosity into action. Only one, at the most two, of the many lives nestled inside our multifoliate seed-casings will ever have a chance to unfold into visibility.

Benjamin brings the *Chronicle* to a close with a short series of fragmentary notes: "Diabolo/The desk at which I did my schoolwork/Neubabelsberg railroad station/Schloss Neubabelsberg." Childhood writing, trains, castles. There is always more to write. The diabolo is a child's toy, two half-cups that run along a string, and Benjamin always loved toys. Neubabelsberg? A suburb between Berlin and Potsdam. The usual Schloss, beneath which they used to exchange spies during the Cold War. An excellent movie museum and a long history of movie-making. Babbling about a new Babel. What could be better for a translator interested in messianic language? I'm sorry he never got back to it, but railroad stations and castles will surely return, like the rediscovery of an old movie, a silent film or an early talkie, to haunt us here in the café.

5

History

The importance of the café in Vienna is indisputable, far more verifiable than metaphysical truth. This, after all, is where doting parents still tell their young children bedtime stories of the illustrious times of the famous Herr Ober Hermann, with his lacquered table of the twenty colors of coffee that his customers preferred, but which have—like all things of the flesh—passed like the strong fist of a blustering autumn wind. Give me a 3! An 18 for me, bitte! The good old days when the precision of the ratio between coffee and milk was considered an art, a link of trust between proprietor and customer. Now precision occurs, all too often, just at the digitized cash register or the handheld credit-card processor, linked invisibly to who knows what command central? Customer service has become the computer server. But don't worry, I won't get on that hobbyhorse. Vienna is too fascinating for me to get distracted by mere economics.

Alfred Polgar said of the inhabitants of the famous Café Central that they were for the most part misanthropes whose aversion to other people was as acute as their need for people: who wanted to be alone, but must have company at hand in order to do so. The habitué of the Central is a person who derives no sense of belonging from his family, profession, or party; the

Café Central comes to his rescue, inviting him to join and escape. Its customers know, love, and underestimate one another. Even those who profess not to know each other regard this non-relationship as a kind of relationship; mutual dislike serves as a unifying force at the Central, a sort of camaraderie. Everyone knows about everybody. The Café Central is a village in the center of the metropolis, steaming with gossip, curiosity, and slander. But this steam, in places like the Central, is just the energy that becomes art in its many forms.

Just think of the enormity of Vienna's contribution to the 20th century: Freud, Musil, Schiele, Klimt, Loos, Kraus, Schnitzler, Kokoschka, Zweig, Schoenberg, Wittgenstein, both Mahlers, Hofmannsthal. The list goes on and on. All of these men became artists because of their imaginations, their fingers, and their vocal cords flowered in the life of the Viennese cafés.

Kubrick's *Eyes Wide Shut,* a dull movie if ever there was one, is a remake of the *Traumnovelle* of Arthur Schnitzler, which is not dull. It was the 20s and Carnival season, always a moment of dissipation of the norms of normality. Fridolin—no wonder they had to change the names in the movie—was bored with his life and his marriage with Albertine. (Nicole has a nicer ring to it, don't you think?) Everything has begun to feel unreal, as if he were in an enchanted world, trapped by the spell of an evil magician. He attends the death of a patient, puts off the daughter's advances, begins to wander the streets, meets a kind whore named, what else?, Mizzi, and then nips into a cozy little coffeehouse for a late night comfort cup.

An old pal, Nightingale, arranges for him to gain entrance to an aristocratic villa and a costumed debauch—with the password "Denmark," a word related to his wife's fantasy of a handsome young lover on the Danish coast. He enters the zone of the erotic through her libidinal economy. The woman lays down the template of desire, and, because he is excluded from it, he has something of a psychotic break.

While the others go at each other in the secret Gothic villa, naked but for their masks, Fridolin's identity is uncovered and a woman has to pay the ultimate price for his...his what? Greed? Dissatisfaction? Lack of magic? Stupidity? This is about as far from the Orphic orgy as one can imagine. It is what occurs, once the gods have fled, as a vapid substitute for what once was a rite of communion. Fridolin experiences what he takes to be the vacant nullity of time and then thought of driving to some station, taking a train to wherever it might be and vanishing from the lives of everyone who knew him, to resurface somewhere overseas and begin a new life as someone else.

This is a fantasy every man knows: I will become no one, anonymous. That is freedom. Fridolin returns, as the morning light eases over the skyline, to Albertine's bed, where his mask of the previous night's prowling lies on the pillow. It's a ghost story, a fairy tale, just like life itself. Misread completely if it's read as realistic fiction, an oxymoron if ever there were one. Schnitzler was tracing the contradictions in Viennese society that would lead to a huge crash whose after-shocks we are still feeling, still living out. Something just beneath the surface was already beginning to crack the marble tabletops, to spoil the brewing coffee.

A seismic swarm was occurring. There was the struggle between the founder of Zionism and the anti-Semitic mayor of Vienna, the fading of the legal reforms and the arrival of the seeds of fascism, and then, the disaster of disasters, the contorted little man from the provinces, full of dumplings, who would return in '38 to the Heldenplatz with his Panzer divisions and all those pretty black and red flags flapping against the buildings on the Ringstrasse. The people, most of them anyway, would love the show. They would cheer when the shops were closed. *Gemütlich.*

The whole century was being heated past the boiling point in that fragile white coffee cup that was *fin-de-siècle* Vienna. History, its steam smashing the cup into little bits and pieces, tiny shards of porcelain, was a volcano ready to blow and there was an infinite disparity of scale between the warm cup of pleasure, reading, and companionship, and the forces on the march through the Reich. The seismologists—Benjamin, Schnitzler, Kracauer, and many others—knew what was to come, but didn't, even with all that intellectual ability, have the resources to put a halt to its approach. Why is that? How does it happen that the most intelligent people of a country are run out of town by a rabid little dog, like some sort of mangy Texas mutt leashing the world to the squeak of his little bark?

The aroma of coffee, sadly, met its temporary limit there in the Platz of the Pretty Buckles and at the Hotel Imperial, where the little man spent the night. Even the best brew from the finest bean, even the most elegant wood-grain espresso, even the warmest of conversation across the table, cannot—not on its own—stop the emergence of the kind of bondage that the men with armbands and shiny visors brought so violently into Vienna. For that to stop, for that barbaric cruelty to vanish from the earth, all the men and women in the cafés will have to continue to think, to write and paint, compose music, to talk and to organize. And sometimes to take to the streets. Otherwise, coffee will lose its magic forever and simply become a drink among other drinks: without distinction, without history, and without vision. If that occurs, then we are all lost, and might as well become a faux barista at a fast food joint, where the word barista should never be spoken. This is the bleakness of absolute winter.

I was once a guest at a training session at the Hotel Sacher, where, after they bowed and handed us our complimentary copy of a little booklet called *Das Wiener Kaffeehaus Heute,* the very officious officials handed us a list of terms to memorize and we were required to recite it, in the proper order with proper definitions, before we were allowed to enter the hotel's restaurant for dinner with the other guests. It was absurd and aggravating, but effective.

Here, from memory, is an abbreviated version of the list:

Grosser Schwarzer: large black

Kleiner Schwarzer: little black

Grosser Brauner: large brown

Kleinere Brauner: little brown

Verlängerter: an extended cup, that is, weaker

Fiaker: *Verlängerter* with rum and whipped cream

Melange: a mixture with egg-yolk and honey

Cappuccino, or *Kapuziner*

Mazagran: with ice cream and a cherry and sometimes with rum

Einspänner: a "one-horse carriage," black in a glass with a freshly whipped cream

Eiskaffee: with vanilla ice-cream and lots of *Schlagobers*

Maria Theresia: black coffee with orange liqueur and whipped cream

Pharisäer: like an Einspänner, but with rum

Franziskaner: Melange with whipped cream and chocolate flakes

Margiloman: mocha with cognac

Türkischer: thick as mud, but far more delightful to the taste-buds

Espresso: the usual, in the Italian style

This is, I admit, a vast simplification of the Viennese system, but how could it be otherwise, since every system is a simplification?

Even the Official Coffee Legend of Vienna and Herr Franz Georg Kolschitzky, as I have mentioned, is awash in strife, for historiography is always a field of battle. Karl Teply, an expert in the recondite art, discovered in the archives that there was an imperial license from 1685 that gave the brewing and serving rights of the 'Turkish drink' to one Diodato—which means, quite aptly, a gift of God—an Armenian leader who opened the first café in Wien at 14 Rotenturm Square.

The Ottoman soldiers were bearing down hard on Vienna, where, as the official legend has it, Kolschitzky passed secretly through the Turkish lines to bring reinforcements just in time and was rewarded with some of those mysterious dark beans left behind by the retreating forces. Apparently, this is just a myth concocted for the usual reasons, to banish the infidel (however imagined) and to uphold "our" dignity. It does seem, however, that regardless of Diodato, Kolschitzky was indeed the first genius to add milk to coffee, thus forever changing the taste of the world.

Scratch the surface of Vienna and there is a history of its cafés and their links to the great modernist innovations. The Griensteidl with its *Jung Wien;* the Herrenhof and the Hawelka. The great Café Central, ruled over by the lovely old eccentric Peter Altenberg. Without the inspiration of coffee, without those delectably obscene dollops of cream, we wouldn't have had all of this outpouring of words, music, neuroses, and paint. The Viennese coffeehouse gave us the 20th century as we know it.

In 1938, that year of the monster, one Signor Gaggi was making his brilliant innovations to the espresso machine on the other side of the Alps to the south and Hemingway was becoming more and more Hemingway, but when those shiny boots arrived in Austria, coffee was doomed, at least temporarily, for all the cafés had to be "Aryanised." The Nazis, who knew nothing of the art of the bean, nothing at all, handed the cafés over to their thin-lipped, leder-hosened henchmen, who created a catastrophe that we can only bear witness to from an unbridgeable distance:

> Café Mozart, Wiener Künstlercafé, Café Schottentor, Graben-Café, Café de Paris, Café Bristol, the Reiss-Bar, Café Raimund, Café Prince Eugen, Café Gartenbau, Café Sans Souci, Wr. Ringstraßencafé , Café Gross, Café Dobner, Café Westminster, Café Ritter, Café Josefstadt,

Café Maria Treu, Café Bauernfeld, Kaffee Colosseum, Café City, and the Café Klinik.

All of these noble institutions, these cauldrons of gossip and art, were shut down or given to the broken and small-minded. Even the Herrenhof, with its elegant interior and bright neon signs across the front, its luminaries such as Polgar, Kraus, and Broch. All handed over to the *Verwaltung*, the pettiness—the squint and the raised nose—of a deadly bureaucratic administration. All those conversations; all those love affairs. All those Viennese heaps of whirled whipped cream and pastries so sweet that they make your teeth hurt. Closed. Snapped shut with a vengeance.

This is what happens when men arrived who knew nothing of the slow arts of roasting the bean and we've been making sure ever since to open new cafés accessible to all, leaving them open until we're sure the last customer has been served. If only such boys would take up acting at a young age and confine themselves to the theater. Poor theater, to be sure, and a disservice to the art, but at least they would have no command over *weapons*, no sense of *missions* to be accomplished. And after the play, after the curtains had fallen and the young men and women stepped into the swirling snow of the Viennese night, some lonesome and some casting quick eyes at one of their companions, they could all head over, tired but happy, to the Central for one last round of a *Maria Theresia* or a *Pharisäer.* Coffee with whipped cream would have capped their night, would have prepared them for sweet dreams that would not have turned into a nightmare. When Achille Gaggi filed patent 365,726 in the autumn of 1938, at a time when Italy and points north had other things on their minds than the appearance of an improved espresso machine, life was changed. True, this change was not as dramatic as the terrors brought on by the blustering machismo of small, fat men with theatrical pretensions, but in the long run, perhaps equally as important. Signor Gaggi, working quietly in his shop, gave all of us a kind of opening toward life. Go visit their *Robecco sul Naviglio* production plant down in Milan; watch them clean and polish the metal, test the steam nozzles and the computer chips. Size up the TE/TD series, compact but lovely, with two infusion heads, the usual built-in pump and a cup warmer on the top. Absolute beauty; top of the line.

This is the very essence of all technologies: to serve as a pleasure-producing machine. Too bad it doesn't always work out like that—after all Hemingway's story has a lovely steam coffee machine in it; the Panzers worked like a charm; and nuclear blasts rain down with precisely measured rings of destruction. It may well be that it'll be the end of us all, the beginning of the world without coffee, and one with very little chance that the next evolutionary experiment will lead back to the roasted bean, a miracle in itself. Think of all the wonders, accidents, thefts, amorous partings, sweaty palms, heart-breaks, sacrifices, and deaths that it's taken for the bean to move from Abyssinia to the Orphée.

The little Museo Gaggi at the plant in Milan boasts coffeemakers from 1948 to the present, photos of Gaggi with Presidente Leone and of the Sirroca Bar in London, and as much free coffee as you can drink in the short walk around the exhibit. The history of the bean and its carrier, the café, were brought to the edge of annihilation by the fat little actor's henchmen, their polished arrogance, their uniformed stupidity. But Gaggi and Hemingway were working away on other projects, projects that would survive the war and extend toward the future, and the Viennese café owners returned to clean up the rubble, lay down new tablecloths. That's the hope of history.

6

Ghosts

Philosophy is the preparation for death. Life is being-toward-death. That's what they say and then an old king appears, a fluttering shade as if from nowhere. Jean-Paul Sartre, almost forgotten now, but once not so very long ago he was the high priest of the philosophy of the Parisian persuasion, worshipped by millions. I, however, have a score to settle with him, for he maligned the magnificence of the common waiter and this is well-nigh unforgiveable.

Writing of those who served him at the Deux Magots, he complains that the waiter's movement is quick and forward, a little too precise, a little too rapid. He comes toward the patrons with a step a little too quick. He bends forward a little too eagerly; his voice, his eyes express an interest a little too solicitous for the order of the customer. Finally, he tries to imitate in his walk the inflexible stiffness of some kind of automaton while carrying his tray with the recklessness of a tight-rope-walker by putting it in a perpetually unstable, perpetually broken equilibrium which he perpetually re-establishes by a light movement of his arm and hand. All his behavior seems to us a game: little bit too much of this, a little bit too much of that. Too quick, too eager, too solicitous. So says Jean-Paul.

This is a caricature with which we are all familiar, that of the supercilious Parisian waiter who must, at any cost, humiliate his clientele. He is the resident sadist in the café and the indolent masochist in the bedroom. This is the young waiter in a hurry, who believes that speed is the essence of superiority. Soon enough, life will teach him otherwise. His hair is slicked back, as if he were a movie star, and he believes the towel is to be used to flick rather than to wipe.

Undoubtedly there are those in the profession that more or less fit this ridiculous image, but most eventually grow out of this immature stage of service. They learn, usually after years of hard work and getting to know their customers more deeply, that it is the work itself that is important and not their personal style, much less their own lives outside of the café.

And then Sartre has the gall to complain that, to the imaginary waiter, his work seems like a game. Well? As he himself goes on to point out at great length, none of us can do anything but play at being this or that, whether a waiter or a philosopher. We all play roles, act out a play without an essence, put on costumes that can never be our own. Isn't that what writing itself is? It is true that sometimes we long to be at one with ourselves, to put on the cloak of our jobs and seamlessly become that cloak. I am the waiter. I am the flight attendant that speaks to you like an automaton. I am the Prime Minister. I am the writer. And it is also true that we should resist this impossible temptation. We cannot be what we are and we are what we are not: this is the structure of the imagination. Again, fine. We improvise ourselves, we learn the gestures of our professions. We learn to play the play.

But in my experience, waiters are among those who know best how to play this play as if there were no exit from the role. Haven't you tried, now and again, to get a waiter to break out of that role? To try and see around the corner of the presentation of today's special toward some out-of-context personality? But waiters know better than to break the role while working, for, while working they belong to the café, they give themselves absolutely to the play of the café. That is the great work. Wherever we find ourselves, we have to play the work, to become the artists of our own lives. Sartre, of course, knows this, so he shouldn't have picked on the waiter. And just a few paces away, the Café Flore would have gladly accepted him as an apprentice waiter or as a patron, a role that takes practice to perfect as well.

Waiter-patron is a dialectical composition, and, as such, the one cannot be without the other. Each must take a position so that an exchange can occur, an exchange of money and coffee, of bantering, of occasional irritation. So that each, in that context, might be itself and hold steady, in a highly provisional way, in the flux of experience. Each is subject-object in its turn, for the other, but neither is a being-for-itself, apart from relationship. It is not, it is true, dialectical in the Hegelian sense, for there is no *Aufhebung* that will raise, cancel, and preserve the other into a new form, but in a more modest sense that the space of commonality is preserved only by maintaining the differentiations of role. As roles, they can of course be exchanged as well, as many waiters go after work to order lattes at other cafés and many patrons leave the café for their jobs at a restaurant.

Perhaps Sartre should have even stuck to weather-watching and the management of his balloons. The philosopher as professional meteorologist is something we have not yet seen enough of and philosophy itself gives us nothing much about the weather. At least with the meteorologist, we get information and predictions, utilitarian help for the next day. Shall I carry an umbrella or take my sunglasses? A sweater or a jacket? Check the weather and then decide. How can philosophy offer us the scent of coffee, the cup warm in our hands, since all too often it is in a rush to move beyond the so-called particular—but this name already gives the game away—to a more general form of existence via the high road of abstraction. Perhaps literature is better at that? A granting of the sensuous particular?

Ernest Hemingway once wrote a short little narrative called "A Clean Well-Lighted Place," and I know, or at least think I know, what the old waiter in that story is feeling when after his shift at the café ends he goes to another bar down the street and admires the shining coffee machine. We all love shiny things. For the old waiter, who has become unhurried in his movement, the shine had worn off most things, a loss that allowed him to see through the brusque impatience of his younger colleague and take note of the dignified sorrow of the man, even older than he himself, who was one of the regular patrons in the café.

These regulars, which every café always has—even if the 'café' is simply a table shoved out onto a cracked and uneven sidewalk with a couple of plastic chairs with torn seats—are always fascinating. It's the old men who gather together to remember, to joke, to play dominos, and to await the end among friends while their wives gather in kitchens or beauty salons to do much the same. It's the *Stammtisch*, the table of ancestors, where the old men come to play *Scharfkopf*, drink a few, kibbitz. The same things, night after night, happen in the same ritualized way.

> It was late and every one had left the café except an old man who sat in the shadow the leaves of the tree made against the electric light. In the day time the street was dusty, but at night the dew settled the dust and the old man liked to sit late because he was deaf and now at night it was quiet and he felt the difference. The two waiters inside the café knew that the old man was a little drunk, and while he was a good client they knew that if he became too drunk he would leave without paying, so they kept watch on him.

Inside, there are the old waiter and the young waiter, the unhurried and the hurried, both of whom know how to keep an eye on the customers. A soldier and his girl scurry by outside in the streets, the light shining off the brass number on his collar and both of them anxious, in different ways, about what the night might bring. And there is the deaf old man, habitually drunk on brandy and able to feel all the subtle differences between night and day. Just last week he had tried to hang himself, but nonetheless he has returned for another drink at the late-night café. "He was deaf and now at night it was quiet and he felt the difference." Just a series of letters on a page. *Nada*, really. He tugs on our hearts and we all want to meet him for a nightcap.

Before he became Papa, Hemingway was only a nineteen year old boy full of shrapnel and longing for Agnes von Kurowsky, the woman who nursed him back to health after he was wounded on the Italian front in 1918. No man can resist a woman in white caring for him when he's been condemned to a stint in a bed with clean sheets. She, however, wasn't interested, so he proceeded to fall for one gal after another. I don't remember the grand total. He should have stayed in Italy, learned the language, and—twenty years later—gone to work writing publicity copy for Signor Gaggi. Milan could have been the city of his love, although it, too, would have become treacherous for foreigners, those with a streak of decency or with an interest in modern art.

Hemingway could have lived calmly, without the drama of Paris and the Spanish bullfights, without Key West and the Finca Vigia. Without the safaris in Africa and the last explosive blast of the old double-barreled Boss in Ketchum. Then we would have had the strange genealogy of D'Annunzio, Pirandello, Marinetti, Svevo, Montale, Levi, Hemingway, Pavese, Moravia and Morante, Ginzburg, Calvino, Eco, Calasso, and Mazzotta. All the famous Italian writers. Deep in his cups of wood-roasted coffee at the Caffé Sant' Eustachio in Rome—opened the same fateful year that Signor Gaggi started his operation to the north—he could have, in his deep operatic baritone, belted out Apollinaire's words:

> You are in the garden at the inn
> You are completely happy a rose is on the table
> And instead of getting on with your short-story
> You watch the rosebug sleeping in the rose's heart
> You went on sorrowful and giddy travels
> Ignorant still of dishonesty and old age
> Love afflicted you at twenty and again at thirty
> I've lived like a fool and I've wasted my time
> And you drink an alcohol as caustic as your life
> Your life you drink as alcohol...

The crowds, especially the women, would have loved him. They always did, for women love artists of all stripes and Hemingway was also desolate and handsome, a fatal combination. He still could have made the novellas as bitter as a dark roasted espresso.

"For what?" That's the question that the old man and his friend, the old and unhurried waiter, are thinking about without thinking about it. As they walk down the street in the fresh light of the morning, in the dusty afternoon, or late at night when the dew has cooled the evening air. "For what?" We live unprotected. Hadley lost the bulk of his other work on a train to Lausanne in 1922. Another train headed in the wrong direction. Where did those typed pages end up? Where is the SBB lost and found? Somebody must have called.

"I am of those who like to stay late at the café," he said. "With all those who do not want to go to bed. With all those who need a light for the night. Each night I am reluctant to close up because there may be someone who needs the café." I am with the waiter and the old deaf man with his nightcap, with "all those who need a light for the night." We all need a nightlight, for there is a 12-gauge always close at hand.

Sometimes the destruction rains down on a whole people, sometimes the shotgun is a nuclear blast, whether accidental or intentional. Neither literature nor philosophy seem to be able to protect us from our own greed and stupidity. Sometimes, after the café is shut down and we wander home through the fog or the buzz of the blurred halogen lamps above, the ancient black hound comes upon us in the quiet hours and takes our throat in its jaws. We can't breathe; our chests contract and cave in. We have to lie down and count our breaths.

Everything feels absolutely senseless and the panic hits the stomach like a firebomb in slow motion. This is the very moment, we know, when we are somehow, for some unknown reason, supposed to battle our fear of oblivion, our terror at being wiped from the table of life like spilled water, and then, like good old St. George in his shining metallic skin, overcome the reptilian breath of the dragon.

After sitting in the darkness being slowly charred by the fire as the pages of our lives curl into ash, we click on a light and in that austere lucidity and reach for whatever is handiest. Tonight it's a citation from Hegel's manuscript of the *Realphilosophie*, 1805-06 and it's all about night. The human being is this night, the large-foreheaded one mutters (surely under the influence of the Dog): this empty nothing that contains everything in its simplicity. This night, the inner lining of nature that exists in phantasmagorical presentations, is night all around. One catches sight of this night when one looks human beings in the eye, into a night that becomes awful. Things appear and disappear, a bloody head and an unidentified white shape fly through the air. The Dog licks its chops.

We conjure what is not-there. That's the miracle of the imagination and this is night. It is because we are this empty nothing that we can contain everything from the sleekness of the Gaggi to the paintings by Vincent or the stories by Hemingway. Everything, to be sure, doesn't come in one fell swoop—we'd never survive that—but is paced and parsed, timed. That which is and that which is not, although how to tell the difference is finally beyond me, comes as an erratic rhythm. The inner and the outer lining of nature folded across one another. From the great and enigmatic world.

The world is full of these burning images; the night is, as it were, taking over the earth. Terror is everywhere. But this isn't fair to night, which has put up with far too much abuse since Hesiod's great-hearted and erotic Night fell into the hands of Socrates and became the symbol for everything that is not ordered and numbered by the laws of light, all because the Day became too proud of itself and wanted to dominate the whole shebang, the whole kit-and-kaboodle.

The shotgun also fired at Chernobyl, in the Ukraine, on April 26, 1986. Boom: an explosion in Reactor #4. Everything died; everyone fled, but disturbing images have since been posted by one Elena Filatova, that beautiful Kid of Speed who has a camera, a motorcycle that flies as fast as a bullet, and a mind that purrs as precisely as the engine of that full-throated pocket-rocket that she rides between her leather-clad thighs. One of the photos, "Ghost Café," especially haunts me. An image from the past, from far away—but not that far away, never that far away—and from the site of disaster.

There it is, just on the other side of a dilapidated tangle of barbed wire. The grass and trees are still there, untended and who knows how genetically twisted, perhaps a vision of all of our futures. The windows are blackened and broken, the sign on the roof unilluminated since that day in 1986 when the meltdown occurred and people stopped going to the café. Many of them went instead to the graveyard, where they will radiate the earth for the next 48,000 years. No more dancing, no more flirtations, no more music. No more coffee. Not here. Never another latte. Only ragged ghosts.

Ghosts inhabit all cafés the world over, including the Orphée. But here, as in the other cafés where coffee is still served, the ghosts come calling upon the living to ask questions, make demands, offer gifts. In the Ghost Café of Chernobyl, however, the ghosts come only to meet other ghosts. There is, as it were, only the ghost of the ghosts. There is no exchange between the living and the dead; it is the dead zone of death, something, perhaps, like the black hole of Tartarus in the underworld. It is the inferno that emerges on the surface of things, the site that radiates the rapid clicks of death and which can only be approached with a Geiger counter in hand and with the approval of the personnel of that administer the Zone of Alienation.

This café falls into a deeper and deeper silence and only by a miracle will it one day speak again. It curves back in time, folding and warping, as the rest of life rushes past it and on into the future. It waits for us with measureless patience, waits for us to measure our miscalculations and the over-stepping of our bounds, as a kind of radioactive memorial. And radioactivity cannot be contained. It breaks its barriers. Who knows how the long term color-coded distribution map of cancer will look? Death breeds more death.

We are all the poor waiters and the supercilious patrons in Sartre's Deux Magots; all of us are Hemingway's two old men and the younger one; the woman and the soldier hurrying toward an assignation; the victims at Chernobyl; and the ones who give witness to the calamity. This is what painting, philosophy, literature, and photography do, regardless of their genre or their objects of contemplation. Each is a witness to the flux, to the passing and the passing away of all things so that something different can appear. Witnesses to our own immense will-toward-death and to our own small, barely audible, cry of hope that we, too, can sit down with one another and talk, drink coffee spiced with a bit of something stronger, in the café that all of us, as nomads, call home.

7

Musing

We slip into the café for the quiet focus that being alone in others' company induces. We come so that body and soul can mend back into each other and then, as if from a gust from outside the warmth of the café, Orpheus, the one who tears everything into shreds appears. The god who is not quite a god, born of Apollo, the one who goes in search of Eurydice, the Thracian nymph fatally bitten by a snake as she was fleeing from the embrace of Aristaeus. It was attempted rape—of course she turned and ran. Who wouldn't? But the snake, as it always is, was waiting.

How do we approach the land of the dead? Or is it the dead who come toward us, silently beckoning? Those shades who have no substance, who are shadows of a memory as insubstantial as the mist that rises from the ground at twilight as the earth cools down from a scorching day. From each and every table in the café, a path winds down toward the underworld. When we step into the café we step from a world of shades outside into a world of shades inside. Can you hear them speaking? I hear the murmur incessantly, always, night and day except when I am dead asleep, out cold, and perhaps even then they are sighing away in the other world. To walk into the land of the dead to find that which we love most deeply and then, turning because we have no choice but to turn, we lose the dead as they fade back into the night.

Orpheus is said to be the first singer. He gathers all of nature into a harmonious whole and enchants the animals to sit at his feet in the cool shade of a leafy tree barely fluttered by the breeze. All is summer. The sky is high and blue. The clouds are whitely piled upon themselves as they reach for the pinnacle of the sky. The heat seeps languidly into our bones and our breathing deepens toward a blissful sleep. The green furze of plants enfolds us in its verdant abundance. This is the happiness of the earth. But Orpheus, at least in this one thing, is like the rest of us poor sods. He can't live, not for long, in the happiness of the summer of the earth. He can't bear the thought of his beloved's death. Somehow, with her death, he has failed in his own life. Our own death is not, finally, all that bad. Not really. There must be an instant of great calm as the end occurs. Just giving in, finally, with a last breath. Just, at last, accepting. Perhaps it's the only moment in which we truly achieve complete surrender.

Why doesn't Orpheus leave us alone? If he gazes at us, at whom is he gazing? The living or the dead? He looks beyond us, through us. I, for one, don't want to be snared in that gaze: predatory, full of the black sun, hopeless. I have struggled with all my might to evade Orpheus, to refuse his gentle invitation that guarantees only a rending without account. It's as if Orpheus keeps prying open a narrow track between living and dying, the sun and darkness, voice and silence, and cannot leave well enough alone.

The night and nothing but the night.

The old legends tell us that Aristaeus was the son of Apollo and Cyrene, a nymph carried off by Apollo for the sake of his insatiable desire. The gods get what they want, when they want it. Aristaeus is taken from his mother as an infant and raised by Cheiron, the Centaur. Not a bad tutor, at any rate, and so the young boy learned the arts of healing and prophecy—like father, like son—and the agricultural arts of beekeeping, olive-growing, and cheese-making. Like so many young men have been known to do, he one day saw a beautiful young woman and began to chase her across the landscape.

As Eurydice fled, she stepped on a snake, which pierced her foot with its poison and she faded into a blue shade passing into Hades. Even in the face of his vast knowledge, Aristaeus's bees mysteriously begin to die, and he discovers from his mother, who is living deep within a spring, that after Eurydice's death Orpheus had died as well. Cyrene instructs him to bind the old shape-shifting Proteus—mirroring Odysseus's task—who tells him to offer bulls as a sacrifice to Eurydice's sisters, who had been causing the bees' deaths, and to Orpheus. Nine days later, he returns to find that the sacrifice has been effective and that the bees are now swarming in the rotting carcasses of the bulls.

Aristaeus, broken but still living, leaves the mainland of Greece, marries the daughter of Cadmus of Thebes—but there's another story—and has a son, Actaeon. You know his fate after lifting the heavy fronds around the pool's edge and gazing upon Diana at her bath. Torn, like Orpheus, to shreds. His death destroys Aristaeus—grief seems to be passed down from generation to generation—who then becomes king of Sardinia, and, in some of the versions, of Sicily. Taking his bee-lore and wine culture throughout the Mediterranean, he eventually came to be worshipped as a god and then vanished from the sight of mortals. But here he is again.

Orpheus is son of Apollo and the muse Calliope, so the Lyre-Player and Aristaeus are half-brothers. He accompanies the Argonauts, teaches them the Mysteries, protects them from the Sirens with the twanging of his lyre, loses Eurydice, recovers and loses her again, and ends his life torn to pieces by the Ciconian women. Like poor Pentheus in drag, torn to shreds bit by bit by his dear birth-mother, death-mother. Apparently, the ladies were a bit put off with Orpheus because he gave up on love in order to live in the memory of his first love. Women despise men who live in the past or who, like Narcissus, cannot turn from their own reflection in the still pools of the forest. Such men come to the café often. The last romantics, they call themselves, deep in their cups. Usually, they are exceptionally bad poets.

The Muses recovered his body, except for his poor severed head, which had floated down the river Hebrus to Lesbos.

They kindly buried it and his lyre took its place in the skies as a constellation, Lyra. Earth and Heaven: all is bound together by Orpheus. The Lesbians, because of their respectful generosity, became skillful in music and produced that great lyric poet of their own, Sappho.

> Come, Aphrodite, and accept these golden cups full of our nectar.
>
> Where is your sacred grove of trees, abundant with ripe apples,
>
> Of altars smoking with lovely incense,
>
> Where all is shadowed by the dark petals of spring roses?

All of these stories echo one another, form a variation upon a variation? No wonder Odysseus becomes the great hero, for he is both the summation of even more ancient legends and the fragmented source for many of the other heroes who come after him. The Ciconians, the Sirens, Proteus. Then there is the dismemberment of Osiris, Zagreus, Adonis, Actaeon. Every man is torn to shreds. Women often are the ones who flail the body from the bones, but women also, Isis or the Muses, are the ones who put the male body back together.

Aristaeus and Orpheus: half-brothers chasing the same woman. The woman separates the men, causing death all around, just as their bodies will have been dismembered by the rage of women on the tracks of Dionysos. What's to be done? Who can listen to the song and survive? What happens when the head and the body are separated and there is no one to sew them back together? How can the burial mound and the heavenly bodies be brought back together? And what happens to woman when she remains a shade, at the beck and call of all those failures on men's parts? Or, like Echo, condemned to be a digital recorder for her beloved. Is Eurydice indeed trapped forever by Hades, or is she, perhaps, weaving her own dark art into which we are all woven?

Eurydice Replies

It is time.

Cast yourself now into the harsh rhythms of presto, agitato,

Hold your pulsing hands steady with just a bit of speed beyond tactus,

For even now Orpheus breathes—

It is a pause,

A trill—

Into the lassitude

A melody that makes a lost afternoon artful,

And there we find in the time between Plato and Virgil,

Eurydice, who dies from the snakes, or passes from dancing with the maenads

At her wedding into an ethereal world and out of reach, becomes

Not an apparition, but a woman:

she who speaks—

Down the throated houses of a tempered memory,

Through the resonant chambers of a body vesseled within and without,

a measured water glass that plays a cappella, wind chimes in the night,

But not quite, not quite:

Those sound waves arc

Around us, mark us. One side of the palm

Then the other, in a flourish life lines sprout from music

Out of the underworld that only breathes its life

In reverse: We can hear ourselves now as we sound

In a life: It is time. One thousand and one

Stories slip from her long braids.

This lyre plays with gut, plays with hands—
Such free movement and today Eurydice replies.
A tongue fills with secrets:
the lowest note sounds far from the center
of her body, a single pitch, reaches out

For all the slivered papers, tasseled with letters,
That carve the portal between the living and the dying,
That can only be read by the initiated,
For those who can hear her speech.

Of that body close to the ground:
One thousand and one stories drift from her long braids.

Eurydice speaks. Eurydice turns on her own volition, in the rhythm of her own revolutions, as, coming and going freely, she passes as she pleases. The stories fall from her braids like waterfalls.

The café is a place of healing. The bees of Aristaeus have helped ripen the grapes of the wine and Orpheus, with Eurydice, is here to provide the music that consoles and inspires. We exist within the space of Orpheus, but couldn't do so without the gifts of his spurned half-brother as well. We are all stung by the bees, but also pollinated, giving birth to beautiful, exotic flowers. They swarm across the meadows blooming with asphodels and lilies, with snapdragons, orchids, lavender, bahinia, the bright roses running crimson and wild. The humming beehive is the soul of the world:

Last night, as I was sleeping
I dreamt—marvelous error!—
that I had a beehive
here inside my heart.
And the golden bees
were making white combs
and sweet honey
from my old failures.

I love these lines, with their hope that the heaviness of our failures—and how heavy they can be—will, through some mysterious process, turn into golden honey. Marvelous error.

Heartbreak hovers in the corners of all cafés, but especially, perhaps, ones like the Orphée that are thresholds between our humdrum everyday world and the land of the dead, where the hope of return is destroyed in less than an instant by the hesitant step, the turned shoulder, the glance back. The café is where divinity intersects the lives of mortals and none of us, not a single one of us, survives this encounter intact. We all try every trick in the book, but we are shredded, flayed alive for the impertinence of living, dismembered by a malicious band of spirit-hounds who brought Orpheus down, and, bit by bit and with the greatest ecstasy, took him apart.

And yet he sings. He keeps singing. Why? Which way, when he looked back, did he turn his head: to the right or to the left? Wasn't it simple greed for power that made Orpheus nick his gaze backwards? To show that he could be the one who destroyed the possibility of love? To prove that he didn't need Eurydice, the woman who knew all his secrets? Orpheus become Narcissus? And what was Eurydice feeling as she, for the second and final time, became the shadow of herself and vanished back into the unreachable halls? Is that where her home had become? How do we learn to make a home where the cave, brush-covered to keep out the ones who only know how to pry, opens into the darkness?

But aren't these the questions of the young, not the questions of the deaf old man drinking alone, however many others sit in the same room with him, in the café? His questions are different: why go on when there is nothing ahead? Nothing but nothing. Why continue with the cheap, garish charade, that Opera Buffa called "life," in which we're all puppets pulled by almost invisible strings that will soon be thrown into the dustbin? And how can one possibly continue to live when, once the dark vision of the desolate heart of existence with its blinding luminescence of a black hole has passed, we are left with only an empty husk and the realization that nothing has ever been anything but an empty husk?

A café can be a shelter against the elements where one huddles in a warm corner while sleet cuts the purple sky with its bitter reminder of the zero at the bone. Or, when Demeter celebrates her daughter's return and all of April is in riotous bloom—the white-blossomed pear tree outside the back window in the little courtyard—then the café becomes an open-air invitation to sit outside and expand to meet the new season. One turns the face up toward the sun as if we, too, are heliotropes.

An old volume of Rilke's *Sonnets*, earmarked and ink-stained, has accompanied me everywhere. It all begins with a tree: "Da stieg ein Baum." A tree rises up in the ear of the listener and the animals come to quietly gather at its base. It's as if they hear their own voices in the wind through the leaves and know for the first time the fur that brushes against the ground, the wetness of the morning ferns, the pressure of air against a wing, and the cool damp darkness below the earth. Water droplets hang off of the brushes of the fans of cedars. A temple springs up within the ear and Orpheus's simple strings, plucked at great intervals, vibrate along column and trunk. All of this is Rilke.

The world sleeps and there is only the slow rhythm of the breath of the god. *Gesang ist Dasein.* The roses and the weeds, the oil crushed beneath the miles of stone, the diamonds waiting to be mined, the prairie grasses and the lichens, the galaxies and the dark matter that shapes the visible world. Simple? Not for us. This breath, this wisp of nothing. And yet, every once in a great while, we can, perhaps, take the smallest of steps into that wind, that draft that blows from the lyre's twanging. Everything around us, everything within us, is this metamorphosis. And, yet: the god leaves us behind when he takes the step beyond the sound of the lyre.

What matters? One thing and one thing only: *praise*. And not even the decay of fruit or of the corpse in its grave can restrain the praise for which Orpheus holds open the doors of the dead. Not all, of course, can accomplish this praise, but only those who have heard a certain type of call, who, with the dead, have eaten of the bright red poppies that I once picked above the theater at Delphi and placed among the leaves of a book. And all this is accomplished through the passage through dread, for that is how we learn to use our voices. The bees and the butterflies awaken.

> Heil dem Geist, der uns verbinden mag;
> denn wir leben wahrhaft in Figuren.

Orpheus binds us together through the figures of the imagination, through the song that binds all things of the world. Everything is *doppeldeutig*, double-meaninged. Nothing is only itself. Rilke knows this listening. Out of the darkness, he writes, something bright appears, perhaps the distant glint of the dead. Things appear, then, almost before we have time to notice, they pass. That is the instant of appearance and disappearance. *Schein*. The sweet taste of the apple, the wine that evaporates on the tongue, whose being manifests evaporation.

The aroma of coffee wafting out the door, causing passersby to smile without knowing, not exactly, why they are smiling.

Rilke thinks the modern, the ways in which we have outstripped the gods and now lay down our own paths, not as a meander through the morning or afternoon sunlight, not as a conversation that dallies over coffee, but as a straight line, paved and graphed on the grid. We are becoming ever stronger, but also, like a swimmer, losing our strength as we go. He returns to Vera, the young girl whose name opens the sonnets, whose death returns time and again as a memorial through the poet's song. She danced, brought with her the spring, listened to the high and distant music that forever changed her. And, then, after a terrible pounding, she entered the inconsolably open door. Inconsolable. And yet the door is open, always open. It greets us with inconsolability and the absolute freedom of the opening.

Out of all deaths, all the inconsolable tearing that we all experience, out of all of that, Orpheus brings a song. That is the miracle. Not absolute knowledge, not salvation beyond time: just a simple song. Even as the love-scorned women were tearing him apart, mangling him, his heart softened. That's the way it goes, isn't it? We either harden or soften in the midst of our suffering. His severed head and the lyre drifted toward Lesbos, and his song lingers even now in dogs and stones, in the cedars, the maples, and the hummingbirds. In coffee, as well, especially in the aroma and the first sip of the coffee. Only because he was torn and scattered can we now become hearers and a voice for the waters, the sky, the peregrinations of the divine bean through the labyrinth of history.

Orpheus: the singer, the sung. The lyre and the severed head, both scarred and bloodied, wash slowly down the broad river and then drift, as if the drifting were endless, across the wide sea. There are winds and storms, tempests that roar across the oceans that span the earth's surface. All the waters of the world pour into that gaping mouth and out pours the babble of all the languages of the world. The eyes, at first as wide as the wide waters, are soon eaten by the glitteringly beautiful and rapacious fish, leaving only the scoured sockets, from which the fish dart in and out, to stare blindly out at the world. Night falls and day is lost forever. Night reigns as all sight vanishes. The finely carved wood of the lyre warps and the strings slacken. "Gegengewicht,/in dem ich mich rhythmisch ereigne." [The counterweight/in which I rhythmically happen.] The single wave-motion of which I am a particle.

I am only reading, only paraphrasing Rilke into poorly measured prose as I sit in the Orphée waiting for it to close so I can head back to the flat, prepare to leave for Hong Kong. Orpheus goes to retrieve Eurydice. The women retrieve his head and his lyre, after his body was buried by the Muses, but who, in the end, will stitch Orpheus back together? Who will retrieve each of us, after the doors have closed?

Eurydice's Sister

I.

Before La Pieta, those well-chiseled figures
That promise to emerge
Centuries later, as hand moves toward
Stone, quarried out on the backs
Of broken men; we must return
Before Mother and Son, before all laps empty

A god who splits
The world into day and night, the nameless figures
Carry bodies over the Styx, spirited away
Freely or driven in chains, it hardly matters.

Charon bends over the lethal vapors, full.
Hand on pole, thrust into and out of the waters,
He marks the laps between the two shores.

II.

Eurydice's sisters hunt for her, unbidden

And dangerous—sliding between the curtains

Of life and death, vapors

For such forms that can never be counted,

Only felt in the body. Such sheerness!

III.

A lone figure, curved and sheathed

By sorrow, drapes over

Eurydice's lap: her disheveled hair askew.

IV.

My hands stroke the shoulders

That lost their way. Bone

Flesh and breath, the rending of an earth

Shall we play the lyre for those who do not return?

Eurydice is taking a new shape, one that only a woman can sing. "Sei allem Abschied voran, als wäre er hinter...." "Be ahead of all parting, as if it were already behind us" like the winter that has just passed. How on earth do we do that? We can't do that. For there is one winter that is so essentially winter that we can only survive by wintering through the winter. "Überwinternd," Rilke writes. Be forever dead in Eurydice so that we can sing the seamless song. Orpheus requires her death, her coming back to the verge of the light, her disappearance. Ahead of all parting? Be: and know the non-Being of all things, the infinite source of our ownmost vibration, so that, just this once, just for this one instant, we can give our wholehearted and unreserved assent.

Everything is incomprehensibly far apart; incomprehensibly near. Those colors, that light weave. The hand that holds the cup and the tongue that tastes. Sing, then, of the coffee tree: praise it. In the silken thread is the whole carpet; in the bean is the warm aroma of the cup and the camaraderie of the café. The vastness of night, the dazzled night, the clapper of the bronze bell of heaven. How does thought, like the taste of the first cup of the morning, leave an after-taste? How do we remember Aristaeus, Orpheus, and Eurydice?

Midnight

Enough, though, of Rilke. Enough of history and painting, of Gaggi and Papa, of shotguns and nuclear accidents. Enough of the ghosts, all the voices chattering like birds in a great tree. Enough of the bees; enough of Orpheus. It's done. It's finished. I'll take the whisky and coffee over to the scarred wooden table and pull my chair to the door to where cobblestone meets wood. I'll step inside the *Café de la Terrasse.* Come the hard rain, the snow, or the bright clarity of the stars, I'll be open to the weather. The night is quiet; the revelers have passed. I greet, without consolation, this immeasurable darkness. Tonight, for as long as the night lasts, I'll breathe in the cold night air. I'll see who drops by for a last, or perhaps even a first, *copita.* I'll wait on this threshold for as long as necessary. I'll let the night flow into every corner of the café and out through the door into every corner of the world. I will welcome any stranger who happens by. Come, sit with me. We'll wait here, together in the night, musing in the dark.

The Café Library

A Select Blend

Apollinaire. *Alcools*. Trans. Donald Revell. Middletown, CT: Wesleyan UP.

Becoming Human. http://www.becominghuman.org/.

Benjamin, Walter. "A Berlin Chronicle," "Surrealism," in *Reflections: Essays, Aphorisms, Autobiographical Writings.* Ed. Peter Demetz. Trans. Edmund Jephcott. New York: Schocken Books, 1978.

——. *Selected Writings Volume II,* Eds. Michael W. Jennings, Howard Eiland, and Gary Smith. Cambridge: Harvard UP, 1999.

Blanchot, Maurice. *The Space of Literature.* Trans. Ann Smock. Lincoln: University of Nebraska Press, 1982.

—— *Writing the Disaster.* Lincoln: University of Nebraska Press.

Clayton, Anthony. *London's Coffee Houses: A Stimulating Story.* London: Historical Publications, 2003.

Coffee Research. www.coffeeresearch.org.

Conrad, Peter. *A Song of Love and Death: The Meaning of Opera.* New York: Poseidon Press, 1987.

Gaggi Coffeemakers. http://www.aa.it/uk/museo.html.

Ghost Café: Chernobyl. www.kiddofspeed.com.

Heering, Kurt-Jürgen, Ed. *Das Wiener Kaffeehaus.* Frankfurt am Main: Insel Verlag, 1993.

Hegel, G. F.W. *Jenaer Realphilosophie. Vorlesungsmanuskripte zur Philosophie der Natur und des Geistes von 1805-1806.* Berlin: Akademie, 1969.

Hemingway, Ernest. "A Clean, Well-Lighted Place." *The Complete Short Stories of Ernest Hemingway.* New York: Scribner's, 1987.

Kochhar-Lindgren, Kanta. *The Eurydice Cycle.* Unpublished manuscript.

Leakey Foundation. http://www.leakeyfoundation.org

Johann Jacobs Museum. http://www.johann-jacobs-museum.ch/english/kaffeekultur.

Machado, Antonio. *Times Alone: Selected Poems of Antonio Machado.* Trans. Robert Bly. Middletown, CT: Wesleyan UP, 1983.

Ovid. *Metamorphoses.* Trans. A.D. Melville. Oxford: Oxford UP, 1986.

Rilke, Rainer Maria. *Sonnets to Orpheus.* Trans. Stephen Mitchell. New York: Simon & Schuster, 1985.

Sartre, Jean-Paul. *Being and Nothingness.* Trans. Hazel Barnes. Pocket Books, 1966.

Schapiro, Mark. "Muddy Waters." *Utne Reader,* Nov/Dec 1994.

Tripp, Edward. *The Meridian Handbook of Classical Mythology.* New York: Signet, 1970.

Van Gogh, Vincent. *The Letters of Vincent Van Gogh.* Ed. Mark Roskill. New York: Touchstone, 1997.

——. http://www.vangoghgallery.com (Collected Works)

Walzer, Tina and Stephan Templ. *Unser Wien: "Arisierung" auf österreichisch.* Berlin: Aufbau-Verlag, 2001.

www.ingramcontent.com/pod-product-compliance
Lightning Source LLC
LaVergne TN
LVHW091011080826
845145LV00003B/1221

* 9 7 8 8 7 9 2 6 3 3 0 1 9 *